The Beginner's Guide to Self-hypnosis

Ursula Markham is a practising hypnotherapist, counsellor and business training provider. In addition to running her own successful clinic, she gives lectures and conducts workshops and seminars in Britain and abroad. She has appeared frequently on radio and television and is Principal of the Hypnothink Foundation, which is responsible for the training of hypnotherapists and counsellors to professional level.

To Philip, David and Chava
With my love

"These success encourages; they can because
they think they can."
Virgil: *Aeneid*, Book Six

The Beginner's Guide to Self-hypnosis
Ursula Markham

ISBN 1-84333-616-2

A catalogue record for this book is available
from the British Library

Published in 2002 by
Vega
64 Brewery Road
London, N7 9NT

A member of **Chrysalis** Books plc

Visit our website at www.chrysalisbooks.co.uk

Printed in Great Britain
by CPD, Wales.

CONTENTS

Chapter		Page
1.	Hypnosis and Self-hypnosis	7
2.	Imagination and Visualization	20
3.	The Starting Point	32
4.	Giving Up Smoking	44
5.	Losing Weight	58
6.	Ongoing Problems	71
7.	Fears and Phobias	87
8.	Emotional Difficulties	100
9.	Performance under Pressure	115
10.	Making Your Future	127
11.	Step By Step to Self-hypnosis	135

1

Hypnosis and Self-hypnosis

Everyone has some aspect of their life that they would like to improve. It may be that they have a specific problem (such as insomnia, nail-biting, or a phobia), or it could be something more general (such as lack of self-confidence or a tendency towards anxiety). Self-hypnosis can help in all such areas – and it is very easy to learn. Not only that, but once you know the technique involved, you can go on to use it when dealing with any problem that may occur during your life.

As you read this book, you will find examples and case histories dealing with the majority of the more common problems helped by self-hypnosis. But even if you feel that your problem is different, there is a section towards the end of the book that explains how to create an appropriate script for yourself.

There are various ways of using the scripts provided: you can read them over and over until you feel you know the content fairly well, then close your eyes and, after the basic technique, repeat them to yourself. This is an adequate way of working but probably not the most effective, as you may not be able to relax sufficiently well if you are worrying about 'what comes next'. You could get someone else to read the script to you, but that means them being available at the appropriate time. The best solution is to have the script (read either by yourself or someone else) recorded on an audio cassette so that you can listen to it as frequently as you wish and at a time that is suitable to you.

Two important considerations need to be made at this point. First, you should never listen to the cassette when driving or using machinery or sharp objects. The ideal, of course, is to find a time when you can relax completely, either in a comfortable chair or on a bed, but because the relaxed state may slow your reactions somewhat, you should not try to perform any other tasks at the same time. Second, if you suffer from epilepsy, it is best to talk to your doctor to ensure that you are a suitable subject for self-hypnosis as, in a handful of cases, it has been found that the altered state of hypnosis can instigate an epileptic fit. It probably would not happen – particularly if your epilepsy is being well controlled by medication – but it would certainly be wise to have confirmation of this.

WHY HYPNOSIS?

Hypnotherapy is probably one of the safest and most effective methods of helping people to overcome their problems. No medication is involved, nothing is done without the consent of the individual concerned, and it can do no harm at all. In fact, the very worst result would be that it did not achieve all that was hoped for – and this is very rare.

Many people have a false idea of what hypnosis is and what it can do. Much of this comes as a result of seeing stage hypnotists on TV, who apparently make their 'victims' perform ridiculous antics of which they are completely unaware. Stage hypnosis is a completely different technique and nothing at all to do with what you will find in this book. Stage hypnosis is all very well as a form of entertainment with audience participation, but you should remember that not only are the subjects natural extroverts, who would be quite happy dancing on a pub table or making fools of themselves at a party; but also what you see on television is the last part of a process that has been going on for some time, during which the hypnotist can assess who (of about 50 volunteers) will be a good subject and who will not.

So what about hypnosis when used as a therapy – what does it do and how does it work?

The state of hypnosis (whether induced by yourself or by a

professional therapist) is a completely natural one. In fact, you enter that state spontaneously at least twice a day – just before falling asleep and just before waking. It is a state of true relaxation, when it is possible to address the subconscious as well as the conscious mind.

Your mind has two parts: the conscious and the subconscious. It is the conscious mind that can reason and evaluate, and that appears to make all the decisions. But by far the most significant is the subconscious mind, as no decision can be implemented unless the subconscious mind agrees and desires it. And, should there ever be a conflict between the desires of the conscious and the subconscious mind, the subconscious will win every time. Think of the people who try to use willpower (conscious mind) to stop smoking or lose weight. Willpower may see them through for a few days – or even a week or two – but unless they learn to convince their subconscious that they really want to give up cigarettes or to change their eating habits, they will not succeed in the long term.

Our subconscious minds have frequently been 'programmed' (rather like a computer) by people and events in our lives – usually when we were very young. And, just like a computer, unless something is done to alter that programming, it will remain in place.

This doesn't mean that those around us have been malicious or have wished to harm us in any way. Sometimes they may have been so caring and over-protective that they have convinced our subconscious that we are incapable of functioning adequately on our own. Take, for example, the case of a small boy who knocks over his glass of milk so that it spills, and makes a mess on table and floor. Most children do that at some time or another. *But* if on every such occasion the mother makes a great fuss and reminds her son he has to be careful not to drop the glass of milk, she begins to make him anxious – and therefore much more likely to have another accident. As time goes on, her son becomes convinced he is clumsy or accident-prone – an impression often reinforced by his mother, who even tells other people not to give her son things that can break or be spilled because he isn't to be trusted with them.

In that example, the loving mother, who probably wanted to avoid having to wash child, clothes and floor, meant no harm. Yet damage was done to the child's inner impression of himself and, because to a small child grown-ups are always right, he grows up to consider himself an accident-prone individual. That is what happens when the subconscious mind is programmed in a negative fashion at a very early age. It is only when that subconscious mind is deliberately accessed later on that those inner thoughts can be altered.

Your subconscious mind is extremely powerful and it never stops working. When you go to sleep at night, your conscious mind shuts down – but your subconscious remains alert because it is responsible for making your heart beat, your blood circulate and all your other organs continue to function. If your subconscious ceased to work, you would die. And it will continue to work, whether you do anything about it or not. But, since it is there and it is functioning, why not make the best use of it?

Think of your subconscious mind as a giant filing system, containing information about your whole life – everything you have ever seen, heard, felt or done. You may not remember all these things consciously, but they are all there in that filing system and can be recalled by means of hypnosis, should you wish to do so (although total recall is not necessarily needed in order to make the changes you desire).

Some years ago I took part in a hypnotic experiment involving several recruits to the special constabulary. As part of their training process, these people (about 15) were shown a film depicting a bank robbery. The film lasted about five minutes and, when it was over, the recruits were asked a series of questions designed to test their powers of observation. Most of the recruits did fairly well, but there were three, somewhat vague, questions that none of them were able to answer.

Three of the recruits were taken into another room and hypnotised. While under hypnosis, they were asked to 'see' the film again in their imagination. This time, of course, they knew in advance the questions that had been asked. By using this method, all three of them were able to answer those questions – and answer them correctly. Their conscious minds may formerly have forgotten what they had seen, but their subconscious minds had not.

The subconscious mind is the ruler of our emotions and it is up to us to control it, rather than have it control us. For example, if I were to lay a plank of wood about 60cm wide on the floor and ask you to walk along it, you would probably have no difficulty in doing so. If I were to place that same plank of wood between two objects about four metres above your head and ask you to walk along it, I doubt that many of you would do it. Why is this? Because your subconscious mind has already absorbed feelings of fear from all those times when, as a child, you fell off or over something and perhaps hurt yourself. So now, as the seat of your emotions, it sends out messages of fear and you respond by feeling that you could not possibly walk along that plank.

So part of what is involved in learning self-hypnosis is learning how to take responsibility for controlling your subconscious mind. As a practising hypnotherapist, many patients on their first visit have questions they want to ask, fears or misunderstandings they would like cleared up. Here are some of the most common ones – with their answers:

• Will I be asleep or unconscious?
No, at all times you will be conscious and able to hear and understand everything that is said.
• Can I be hypnotised against my will?
Never. If you decide you do not wish to be hypnotised, no one can make it happen.
• What will it feel like?
It is a lovely, relaxed feeling. The closest comparison is to think of what it feels like to be lying comfortably in your bed at night, not quite asleep but almost drifting off. In that state, should there be an emergency of some sort, you would immediately be fully awake and alert, but if all remains calm, you will lie there, quite contented, until sleep comes to you.
• Can I be made to do things against my will?
No, you can only do things with which you are happy to co-operate.

- Which problems can be helped?

Stress, lack of confidence, smoking, weight problems, anxiety and panic attacks, fears and phobias, PMT and menopausal problems, migraine, asthma, exam/interview/driving test nerves, poor memory, pregnancy and childbirth, dealing with bereavement... and much, much more. In fact, any problem that is not purely physical in origin can be relieved.

- Who is a suitable subject for hypnosis?

It is often thought that people who are intelligent or who have a strong will are difficult to hypnotise. On the contrary, these are the people who often make the best hypnotic subjects. With just a few exceptions, anyone who is willing to play their part and co-operate in the process will be a good subject. Those few exceptions are: children under the age of five; some people suffering from epilepsy, as already mentioned; anyone whose mental capacity does not allow them to concentrate on what is being said and to co-operate with it.

- Is the process safe?

Hypnosis can do you no harm at all. The very worst that can happen is that nothing will happen.

- How will I be hypnotised?

Forget the image of the swinging watch. The hypnotherapist will simply talk to you, taking you gently through a process of relaxation (not unlike basic yoga) until you are comfortable enough for their words to reach your subconscious as well as your conscious mind.

Bearing in mind the answer to the last question, you can understand how, with the information given in this book, you will be able to hypnotise yourself. I will tell you the words to say – both for the initial induction process and then for the method of dealing with your own particular problem – and these words will be spoken by you or another person (preferably on audio cassette). It will be just like having your own private hypnotherapist at hand, ready to help you whenever you need it.

TALKING TO YOURSELF

We all talk to ourselves regularly, whether we realize it or not. Sometimes we speak the words aloud, while at other times we simply allow thoughts to come into our minds – or perhaps we use a combination of the two methods.

And we pay far more attention to what we say to ourselves than you might think. The timid person will say, 'I can't', while the determined one will say, 'I can'. And the more we repeat those words to ourselves, the more self-fulfilling they become. Every time the shy person tells themself, 'I cannot face going into a room full of people I do not know', that fact becomes more of a reality, the problem greater, and the negative feelings associated with it more intense.

Think of the thousands of pounds advertisers spend trying to persuade us to buy their products – and they do it by repeating certain words, phrases or slogans over and over again. These people are not fools: if this repetition did not work, they would not spend such fortunes when promoting their goods.

If constant repetition works for marketing people and advertisers, it can work for us too. If we are going to listen to our internal conversations, surely it makes sense to tailor them so that the words used help us to overcome our problems and achieve our aims. It is simply a case of learning to substitute positive words for former negative ones. The next important stage is to combine such words with the use of your imagination and with visualisation techniques – but more of this in the next chapter.

Many years ago, it was thought that it was enough to repeat positive phrases in order to make the desired changes in yourself. And while it is true that these repeated phrases (or affirmations) can be very helpful, they are only a small part of what we now know as self-hypnosis. This is because experts in the field of learning have found that, on average, we absorb:

- 20 per cent of what we read;
- 30 per cent of what we hear;
- 40 per cent of what we see;
- 50 per cent of what we say;
- 60 per cent of what we do;
  But
- *90 per cent of what we see, hear and do.*

As you progress through the book and begin to record your

own audio cassettes, you will find you are making use of all the
ingredients that go to make up that 90 per cent.

- You will *see* the printed words as you read them.
- You will *say* them as you record them onto the cassette.
- You will *hear* the words as the cassette plays.
- You will *do* by turning those words into images in your mind, while listening to the cassette.

In this way, you will be giving yourself the greatest possible
chance of success.

WHERE ARE YOU NOW?

Before you can go forward and work towards making effective
changes in yourself and the way you live your life, you need to be
certain of where you are and who you are at present.

We have already seen that it is necessary to take control of your
subconscious mind and, in effect, to give it orders. Although your
subconscious generates your inner energy, it is your conscious
mind that is needed to plan the direction that energy should take.
The subconscious cannot do this and indeed will continue with
existing habits until you decide to do something to break the pattern. This applies, whether those habits are as basic as which shoe
you always put on first or as life-changing as how you react to the
various emotions demonstrated by other people.

Anyone who can drive a car will have had proof of the way in
which the subconscious takes over when performing a regular
task. All of us have travelled regular and familiar routes and yet,
when we arrive at our destination, we do not actually remember
various parts of that journey. We must have made the correct
turns, stopped at the red lights, avoided the other vehicles we
encountered; and yet we have done so without being consciously
aware of it.

MAKING CHANGES

Human beings have a natural resistance to making changes in their lives. Even those who are in unhappy situations, or who have habits they know it would benefit them to change, find it easier to stay with what they know than to set out to make those changes. And yet, once they have made up their minds and made a personal commitment to change, they are likely to find that it is far easier to accomplish than they previously thought.

Any habit can be changed, but not overnight. It does take a little time and regular effort. The general consensus of opinion is that it takes about three weeks to change a habit permanently. If you want to prove this to yourself, try the following:

Suppose, for example, that you always keep your waste-paper basket to the left of your desk. If it is always in the same position, you can probably toss pieces of paper into it without even having to look at it. Now try changing the position of that waste-paper basket so that it is to your right. For the first few days, you will throw all your rubbish onto the floor on the left. Gradually you will become used to throwing it to the right but you will still have the occasional lapse when, perhaps because you are concentrating on something else, old habits come to the fore and you throw those pieces of paper to the left once more. By the time three weeks have elapsed, however, it is doubtful whether you will ever make a mistake, because by then your subconscious will have formed the habit of throwing rubbish to the right.

The same thing happens when you want to change any aspect of your personality. In the beginning, you will have to concentrate extremely hard. Then you will go through a period of having occasional lapses, but by about three weeks after starting, that change will have become permanent – provided, of course, you have gone about reprogramming your subconscious in the right way. To do this, you need to understand your current position and to be certain of just what changes you wish to make.

Think about yourself
Why not begin by thinking about what you like and what you do

not like about yourself? Make a list, if it helps to write things down. Depending on whether you are in a positive or negative mood when compiling this list, one is likely to be longer than the other. With most people, the list of 'don't likes' tends to be much longer than the 'likes'.

First, take a look at those aspects of your personality that you like. Imagine you were reading this list as if it applied to someone else – someone you had not yet met. Based on that list alone, you would probably think the unknown person was quite reasonable; you might even like them. Add to that the fact that this imaginary someone was obviously trying to change some of the negative aspects of their personality; you would probably find that quite admirable too.

So, before you even begin to make those changes, you can think of yourself as quite a likeable person, who is about to do their best to make themselves even better. I wonder how many times you have thought of yourself that way – or have you just concentrated on your negative traits? Now go on to look at the negative aspects of your personality – we all have them. How many of them are either the result of someone else's opinion of you, or several different ways of saying the same thing? In the first instance, it is necessary to remember that although the other person's words may not be correct, if they are repeated frequently enough, you will come to believe them.

One of my patients had recently come out of a 12-year marriage during which her personality had changed considerably. Her ex-husband had spent most of those 12 years telling her how stupid she was – not always in an angry way, but using such comments as, 'Well, it's no good trying to explain this to you, you'd never understand – you're too stupid.' This woman may not have been a super-brain, but she certainly was not stupid. After hearing those words, day in, day out, for 12 years, however, she had come to consider herself in that way. And that was what she put on her list of 'don't likes' – 'I am stupid'. But this was just the opinion of someone else who, probably to make himself feel cleverer, continued to belittle her at every opportunity.

Sometimes several items on that list of 'don't-likes' will in actual fact be different ways of saying the same thing. Suppose, for example, you have written that you are 'shy', that you 'find it difficult to talk to people' and you are 'a poor conversationalist'. Those three statements are, in fact, just different ways of saying that you are uneasy with people you don't know very well. Bearing that in mind, perhaps your list of negative points could be reduced before you even begin to work on making those changes.

It also pays to remember that what one person sees as a negative aspect of personality, someone else might see as positive. Some years ago, I remember working with a young woman who had been brought up with her four older brothers. Compared to these hearty and outgoing young men, she felt she was 'dull, boring and mousy' (her words). Yet, when I spoke to two of her brothers, they thought she was 'sweet, feminine and gentle'. So it might pay to ask yourself whether what you consider to be your bad points are those that might appeal to other people.

Be specific
When compiling your final list of things about yourself you want to change, it is important to be specific. There is no point just wanting to be 'better', 'nicer' or 'more confident'. You need to be able to specify what it is you want to be better at, in what way you wish to be nicer and, perhaps most important of all, in which areas of your life you wish to display greater confidence.

One of the commonest things people write on their list when I am working with them is that they want to be a more confident person. But what does this mean? How will that increased confidence show itself? It is quite rare for someone to lack confidence in every area of their life. Some may have a quiet confidence at work and yet go to pieces when dealing with relationships. Others may feel positive and assertive when at home, or among family and friends, but have no confidence at all in a work situation.

So do be specific. When making your list, if confidence is one of the areas you wish to work on, ask yourself what it is you will be able to do when you have improved that confidence. It doesn't

matter if there are several different areas concerning confidence
that you wish to work on. You can only deal with one thing at a
time, but having successfully accomplished the first one, you will
find that each subsequent aspect of your life will be easier to
improve.

Why you are as you are
There is a reason for the way you are now – a reason for the good
and bad aspects of your personality. Of course, we each begin
with certain genetic tendencies and aptitudes but, even so, as we
turn from baby to child to adult, it is the people and events we
have encountered in our lives that are responsible for the way we
have developed. Some people will know precisely what words or
events have fashioned them into the adults they are now; others
will have a vague idea; and some will either not have thought
about it until now, or will not have the slightest idea of what has
caused them to develop in a particular way.

And people fall into different categories. To some it is vitally
important to discover the reasons for what they consider to be
their failings. This is not necessarily because they are looking for
someone or something to blame, but simply because they feel
unable to progress unless they have a full understanding of the
background explanation. If you fall into this category, you may
find you need some outside help. While it is possible to discover
a certain amount about the reasons for your current personality
and attitudes, there may be a great deal that your conscious mind
has forgotten and so you will reach a point from which you can
go no further. But, as we have already seen, your subconscious
mind does not forget anything at all and, if accessed, can give you
the answers you seek. To this end, you would be well advised to
arrange one or two sessions with a professional hypnotherapist,
who would be able to help you delve into the recesses of your
subconscious mind to uncover those facts that have escaped your
conscious memory. Then, using the methods outlined in this
book, you can proceed to work on improving the aspects of your
life to which these facts relate.

Other people do not really care why the personality problems in their life have arisen; all they know is that they do not wish to live with them any longer and are prepared to work towards changing them for a more positive way of life. As one of my patients (who was frightened of spiders) told me, 'I don't know what made me terrified of spiders in the first place and I don't really care. All I know is that I am an adult with a problem that I have lived with since childhood, and I don't want to live with it any more.' And that was sufficient for her to be able to use self-hypnosis to overcome that fear once and for all.

A common fallacy
Some people believe – and, indeed, you may have heard it said – that if you remove a negative personality trait without discovering the reason for its existence, another will come in to take its place. I promise you that this is simply not true. Since 1979 I have been helping patients to overcome an enormous variety of problems, and I can assure you that, provided they continue practising the methods you are going to learn until the new habit is firmly entrenched in their subconscious mind, no other problem arises to fill the place of the one that has been eliminated.

OVER TO YOU

You are now entering a truly exciting phase of your life. You have already become more aware of yourself and decided which problems you wish to overcome and, by working through this book and practising the techniques given to you, you are going to achieve your wishes. Just imagine the joy of being in control of your life to such an extent that you can change any aspect of your life you wish and can become the person you truly wish to be. Yes, it will take some effort on your part but, even at this stage, you know that it will be worth while. So take your time... and enjoy the process.

2

Imagination and Visualization

Here is a piece of good news. To make any change in yourself, there is one tool you need that is far more important than any other. And you already possess that vital tool: your imagination. It is your imagination that is going to help you to achieve whatever it is that you want. It is your imagination that is going to ensure you succeed. It is your imagination – and the proper use of it – that is going to put you ahead of about eighty per cent of the population.

Before you say that you are not a very imaginative person or that you find it difficult to 'see pictures' in your mind, remember this: with the exception of those who had the misfortune to be born blind, everybody has a strong and vivid imagination. Or perhaps we should say that everybody was born with a strong and vivid imagination. Many people seem to lose this valuable tool as they grow up.

You only have to watch a child at play and you will be aware of the strength of that child's imaginative powers. Sadly, western education tends to diminish that strength; we are always being taught to think in a purely practical and analytical way when, if only more teachers realized it, the best way of fixing something in the mind is to make use of our ability to visualize it. Consider the difference between being taught history by having to commit to memory lists of events and the dates on which they occurred and being told stories about those same events and dates – stories that conjure up pictures in the minds of the listeners.

I remember taking my sons, when they were quite young, to

Battle Abbey near Hastings. The guide who showed us round the abbey and its grounds was a young university student, trying to earn some extra money during the vacation. At one point we were all sitting on a grassy slope just outside the abbey and the young man described the scene as the Norman army approached, while the English army prepared to do battle. Because of the skilful way in which he told that story, we could almost see the men approaching each other and hear the clash of their weapons as the fighting began. Neither my sons nor I have ever forgotten what we learned that day – all because a young man's skilful and vivid description enabled us to 'see' the whole event taking place.

If you think your imagination has grown weaker because of lack of use, don't worry. You can bring it back to full strength by means of a few simple exercises. Just as any muscle of your body can be strengthened and have that strength maintained by regular use and exercise, so too can the 'muscles of your mind' – your imagination. And since it is such a vital element of self-hypnosis, it is worth taking a little time to ensure that your imagination is at maximum strength before you try and put the other techniques into practice.

HOW TO IMPROVE YOUR IMAGINATION

1. Choose a time when you are unlikely to be disturbed for at least ten minutes and sit in a comfortable chair. Select an item in the room – perhaps a vase, a rug or even the cup in which you had a drink. Look at that item – really look at it. Observe as much detail as you can. Don't just think to yourself, 'Oh yes, that's a vase'. Study its shape, its colour, and any design it may have. Now close your eyes and try to see that vase inside your head, in as much detail as possible. If you find it difficult, don't worry, this isn't an exam – you can't fail. Just open your eyes, study the vase once more, then close your eyes and try again.

The first time you try this exercise, you will probably find it fairly difficult – particularly if you have lost the habit of using your imagination. But persevere and I promise it will get easier.

Then move on to stage two.

2. Once you are able to imagine a specific object, try the same exercise, but this time take in as much of the room as you can see from your chair. Don't just tell yourself that there is a window, beside which are a chair, then a table, and so on. Try and see these things in as much detail as possible in your imagination. Once again, you need to practise this exercise until you are able to do it quite easily.

3. Now it is time to combine memory with imagination. You have proved that you can imagine at will the room in which you are sitting. Select a room from your childhood, or from some time earlier in your life, and see if you can create that room in your imagination. Of course, this time you cannot open your eyes to prove whether or not you are right, but you will find that each time you try this part of the exercise, you will remember more and more until you are able to imagine the whole of the room concerned.

4. The final part of this exercise is to imagine something more nebulous – perhaps a beautiful garden (either real or one you have created in your mind), perhaps a group of trees in autumn, or perhaps a group of people walking along the street. Once you can do this at will (and each stage of the exercise will take you less time with every attempt), you know you have exercised your 'imagination muscle' back to full strength.

WHY IS THE IMAGINATION SO IMPORTANT?

Anything created has first been imagined. An artist looking at a blank canvas or a sculptor contemplating a piece of cold stone can see in their imagination what they are about to create. In the same way, we can 'see' the success we are about to create in whichever area of our lives we have chosen.

It's not necessary to have to have something as tangible as canvas or stone. Think, for example, of champion sprinter Linford Christie. One of the reasons for his great success was that, while standing at the starting block, he could see himself winning the race. You only had to look at the expression on his face to see he knew he was going to do well. And even on those occasions when he may not have been the first to cross the finishing line, he certainly gave his best, often beating his own previous record. All we can ask of ourselves is that we do the best we are able to do – that is what it takes to be a success.

Some years ago I was consulted by a very worried golfer. This man had playing golf for years and had won many cups and trophies. But that particular year, for no reason he knew of, the accuracy of his putting seemed to have vanished. Each time he played, whether in a casual game or in a tournament, he grew more and more anxious as the final shots at each hole approached. And each time he played, his putting seemed to be worse than on the last occasion, until he became so ashamed of his failure at something he used to do really well that he avoided playing altogether.

Of course, in any area of life, what we imagine is self-fulfilling – whether in a positive or a negative way. So, every time this man approached the putting stage of a hole, he began to think 'Oh, please don't let my putting let me down again', 'I hope I manage to putt accurately this time', or 'I mustn't miss the hole today'. All those thoughts were reinforcing the thought of failure in his subconscious mind and making it almost inevitable that his putting would be inaccurate.

Now I know little or nothing about golf, but that did not matter because my patient did. His putting had been so accurate in the past that it had played a large part in his ability to win all those cups and trophies. When he was not feeling anxious, he automatically knew how to stand, how to hold the putter, how much strength to put into the stroke, and so on. My job was to teach him to visualize himself putting the ball into each hole in the way he used to – therefore achieving as much, or more, success as he had achieved previously. He had to do this several times, until he felt completely at ease with the image, before even venturing out onto the golf course. He had to convince his subconscious mind that he was the champion golfer he used to be, and build upon all those years of success rather than worry about the comparatively few incidents of failure. Within a very short

space of time, my golfer was completely back on form again, playing as well, or even better, than ever.

MENTAL REHEARSAL

Think of visualization as a mental rehearsal for whatever it is that
you wish to achieve. Every actor, amateur or professional,
rehearses a part over and over again in order to give as good a
performance as possible on the night. If they rehearse well
enough, by the time opening night comes around, even if they
suffer from nervousness before going on stage, once the performance is under way they know their lines so well that they can
speak them without having to worry about what comes next. And
if they have rehearsed well, they have also 'thought' themselves
into the part so they become the character they are playing.

   This is what the visualization part of self-hypnosis is going to
help you to do. You are going to learn to 'see' yourself in your
mind's eye as becoming the person you want to be and achieving
the aims you want to achieve. Once you have sufficiently
rehearsed to be able to see that end well enough to believe in it,
you will find you do become that person and you do achieve
those aims.

WHAT IS SUCCESS?

Self-hypnosis using visualization will help you to achieve the success you want. But, of course, success means something different
to each individual. Some years ago I was being interviewed on
television about ways of creating success in your life. The inter-
viewer (not a particularly intelligent man) latched onto the word
'success' and said, 'You mean I can make lots of money and have
a big American car and attract all the beautiful women?'. He
could only understand 'success' in a shallow and materialistic
sense and refused to consider it in any other way, however hard I
tried to explain my point of view.

So, what is success? To one person, it might mean being able to contemplate flying in an aeroplane without having to drink themselves into a stupor in order to conquer their nerves. To another, it could mean being able to go confidently into a room full of strangers. To a third, suffering from claustrophobia, it could mean being able to walk as far as the next lamp post.

It is true that, if you learn to become the person you have always wanted to be – gaining confidence, improving your learning ability, getting on better with people – this could lead to such things as promotion, extra money and acquisition of material goods. But these are just pleasant by-products of what you have achieved rather than aims in themselves.

Case study: Esther
One of the greatest success stories I have known is that of Esther, a gentle and somewhat timid woman of 52 whom I met about ten years ago.

It was Esther's husband who first approached me on behalf of his wife. Esther had suffered for years from agoraphobia – an extreme or irrational fear of open or public spaces, leading to panic attacks and reclusive behaviour. The intensity and results of this phobia can vary greatly from person to person. Some live a relatively normal life, provided they avoid wide, open spaces such as country fields or quiet sandy beaches, while others find even going to local shops impossibility.

Esther's condition was the most severe case I had encountered. For the past 11 years she had not been able even to set foot in her own garden. She had become a prisoner in her own home, as everywhere else seemed far too threatening even to contemplate. Esther did not know how it had all started. She had always been quite a shy and timid person but had lived a relatively normal life until she reached around thirty-five. From that time onward, what started as a general feeling of insecurity if she ventured too far from home developed into a phobia so severe that it had crippled her entire life. Can you imagine the misery of feeling too terrified even to set foot outside the back door?

Because of her condition, Esther was not able to come and see me, so in the beginning I used to visit her in her home. She told me she had no interest in discovering how and why this agoraphobia had developed – she just wanted to overcome it so she could live a normal life again.

One thing to bear in mind is that no phobia ever remains static. If nothing is done to overcome it, it is going to get worse. This is because we are constantly reinforcing our own fears. Every time someone like Esther thinks to themselves, 'I really don't like to go outside the house', they are reinforcing that belief about themselves in their subconscious mind. Eventually they become so convinced of the truth of that statement that they actually cannot venture outside.

In Esther's case, we had to go right back to basics. Because of the state she had reached, she was not even able to stand at her own front door if it was open and she could see the world outside. So, having taught her the stages of self-hypnosis that you are going to learn from this book, I suggested to her the image of doing just that – of standing at her front door while it was open, and looking at her front garden and the street beyond.

Remember that she did not have to open the door in reality. She merely had to 'see' the situation in her imagination. And it was important that she did this while she was actually in a place and in circumstances where she felt safe and able to relax. Esther chose to practise her self-hypnosis with the accompanying image when she was in bed at night, with her husband lying protectively by her side. By practising this 'mental rehearsal', night after night, Esther was able to link this feeling of knowing she was safe and secure with the image of standing by that open door. Eventually her subconscious came to believe that standing by the door was in reality a safe and secure thing to do.

Before leaving Esther to practise her self-hypnosis, I asked if, when she felt she was ready, she would do what she had been imagining and open the front door and look out. It was important she did not try to do this too soon but that she should wait until she felt perfectly comfortable with the idea. There is no right or wrong amount of time this process should take. Each person is different – and each stage of the recovery may take a different amount of time.

Esther telephoned me about ten days later, in a state of high elation, to tell me she had now stood at the open front door on three occasions and had experienced no sense of fear or anxiety in doing so. She had rehearsed her part so well in her mind that she had been able to give the performance she desired. That is success. It had nothing to do with money, fast cars or an ideal love life. It was far more important than any of those things because it was the first step for Esther in changing her life forever.

After that we worked on taking three steps down the front path, then back again into the safety of Esther's house. Once that was accomplished, Esther progressed to the garden gate, then eventually down the road, to the local shop, and so on. The final outcome was that, some three months later, a delighted Esther telephoned me to say that not only was she out and about, she was learning to drive.

Personal achievement
It would be very nice for me to be able to say that Esther's success was because of my skill and teaching. But that only played a very small part in the process. All the credit must go to Esther because it can't be easy, when even the sight of the outside world terrifies you, to make yourself practise looking at that world every single day. And as soon as she felt comfortable with one particular image, Esther had to go on to the next one and overcome her anxiety all over again.

However, her perseverance paid off and the rewards for her efforts were numerous. Of course, there was the obvious result that she was able to go out, like other people. This in itself must have changed her life dramatically. She could do her own shopping, visit friends, go out for a meal with her husband – all things that most of us do on a daily basis without even thinking about it. But there was also the sense of having achieved something truly sensational in overcoming the phobia that had ruled (and ruined) her life for so long. This sense of achievement gives an enormous boost to self-confidence, which in turn rubs off on other areas of life. If Esther could achieve what she and many other people would previously have considered impossible, surely there would be no stopping her when it came to achieving things of lesser significance. So I was not at all surprised when I heard that Esther had passed her driving test at the first attempt or that, having offered her services as a helper to a local charity group, it was not long before she was elected to serve on the committee.

Esther's case was one of the severest I have come across, and yet in just three months she was able to conquer it completely and forever, using self-hypnosis and the power of her own mind. So just think what you are going to be able to achieve in the very near future.

FOOLING THE SUBCONSCIOUS

How are we able to fool the subconscious? How is it that by linking security with a hitherto frightening image, it is possible to dispel that fear forever? The answer is that when we do this, we are in fact fooling the subconscious mind. One very important fact to bear in mind is *the subconscious mind cannot tell the difference between what is real and what is imagined*. This means that if you deliberately feed imagined information into your subconscious on a regular basis, it will eventually become convinced that what you have imagined has already happened.

Suppose, for example, you are someone who until now has been terrified of spiders – screaming or perhaps running out of the room should one dare to appear in your vicinity. If on a daily basis you deliberately send images to your subconscious mind of yourself coping in a controlled and efficient manner when a spider is around – until this image feels comfortable to you instead of being something you would like to achieve – your subconscious will believe you have already done so on many occasions. And if this is so – if you are someone who has coped with the appearance of a spider in a calm and rational way so many times in the past – there is absolutely no reason why you should not do so in the future.

Bear in mind that what I said was that you would 'cope' with the situation, not that you would learn to love spiders (or birds, or cats – or whatever else it is that has previously sent you into a panic). If you are someone with a phobia, all you want to do is handle the situation calmly and effectively – nothing more. And that is what self-hypnosis will help you to achieve.

It is quite logical that your subconscious will achieve this result. After all, the fear itself developed into a phobia because, in the past, you have imagined all too successfully how terrified you would be if one of the dreaded creatures came anywhere near you. So you have already proved to yourself that the subconscious mind accepts imagined facts as reality. All you need to do now is send it a different, and more positive, set of facts.

SEE THE FINAL RESULT

Another important point is that, at each stage of your progress, it is essential you imagine a finished, successful outcome rather than some half-hearted stage of being 'a bit better'. If you only imagine some slight improvement in your condition, your subconscious will assume that this is where you want to stop – and a slight improvement will be all that you achieve.

The overweight man or woman must imagine themselves as having reached their target and having become the size and shape they wish to be, as opposed to being a bit slimmer than they are today. The sprinter who wants to improve their athletic performance has to imagine themselves doing as well as it is possible for them to do physically – not just being able to run a bit faster than they can at the moment. The shy individual must imagine themselves coping with meeting a group of new people in precisely the friendly and communicative way they have always wanted to do – not just as entering the room and standing silently in the background instead of turning to flee.

This does not mean that there might not be several stages to your progress. It is vital, however, that at every stage you imagine the final outcome as total success. Even Esther, taking several stages to deal with the problem of her severe agoraphobia, had to visualize each separate stage as being completely successful. When she began by imagining herself looking out of her open front door, if she had pictured herself opening the door, glancing quickly out, then closing the door again (even though this would have been an improvement on her initial reaction), that is where she would have stopped. By picturing herself standing at that open front door and taking a long look at the world outside, her subconscious allowed her to reach that particular point before she attempted to carry out the action in reality.

Case study: Jeffrey
Jeffrey was 35 when I first met him. He was a pleasant and friend-ly man who was doing quite well in his chosen career. He got on well with friends, family and colleagues, but became tongue-tied and terrified when approaching a woman with a view to asking her out. He would blush, stammer, and on the few occasions when he did manage to get the words out, he would do so in such a diffident and awkward manner that he was quite likely to receive a negative response.

The situation had probably come about as the result of one or more scornful or unkind refusals Jeffrey had received when he was quite young. Of course, this is something that happens to a lot of young men when they first begin approaching girls for a date – possibly because they often do so in an awkward manner. Most grow out of this type of shyness but, for some reason, Jeffrey had not.

When Jeffrey first learned about self-hypnosis and how it could help him to overcome his problem, it was vital he imagined him-self being completely at ease when approaching a woman, rather than being slightly less shy than he was at present. Of course, because not every woman wants to go out with every man who asks her, there was always the possibility his offer would be reject-ed. But, even if that were the case, Jeffrey would still have behaved exactly as he always wanted to do and he could therefore still be proud of his success.

DESIGNING YOUR OWN SCRIPT

Throughout this book, when we come to deal with specific situations and how self-hypnosis can help, you will find sample scripts that you can record and use. However, you do not have to copy these scripts word for word. Each individual is different and each of us wants a slightly different outcome, even to similar problems. Therefore the scripts should be taken as a starting point and you may feel free to adapt any or all of them to suit your personality and your particular situation. But if you are unsure about how to vary the script, do feel free to use them just as they are. They are tried and tested, and have been proved to work many times over the years.

So make a friend of your imagination and your ability to visualize. It is a fantastic tool that, when used effectively, will help you substitute what may have been a lifetime of negative thinking for positive thoughts. Enjoy your daydreams because they are helping you to turn wishes into reality.

3

The Starting Point

The first stage in any hypnotherapy session, whether with a professional therapist or on your own, is to learn how to induce what is called the 'trance' state. In truth, I do not really like the word 'trance' as it gives many people the wrong impression of what hypnosis is. It makes it sound as though you are going to lose the power of your own mind, and lose control of your thoughts and actions, when in fact the reverse is true. You are going to use the power of your mind to create the right conditions for the therapy to work. When you are sufficiently relaxed to address the subconscious mind successfully, you have actually measurably altered the function of your brain waves, so for this reason we will use the term 'altered' state of hypnosis.

There are various stages involved in attaining that altered state and as each stage is essential it is worth spending a little time considering how to achieve it.

RELAXATION

Deep physical and mental relaxation is a state that is within the reach of everyone with a little practice, but it is actually achieved by very few. It is often thought that relaxation is anything that does not involve work. In other words, sitting on the sofa in front of the TV or going to bed and having a nap, may be thought of as relaxation. But, while it is true that your body may feel a little less tense in either of these circumstances, it is not what we mean by deep relaxation.

Although it may sound a contradiction in terms, deep relaxation can only be achieved by deliberate effort on your part. And each stage of the process has a reason – which is why it is essential to follow them all in order to be successful. As previously explained, it is only when mind and body are fully relaxed that it is possible for the words used during therapy to reach the subconscious mind; and it is only the subconscious mind that is capable of helping you achieve your aims.

A little later in this chapter you will find the script for creating the appropriate relaxed state for self-hypnosis to be effective, but first there are some important points to bear in mind.

Select a regular time

Where possible, it can prove beneficial to try and practise your self-hypnosis at the same time each day. This is because the mind and body tend to prepare themselves for anything that is a regular occurrence. If you always have lunch at 1pm, you will know that you begin to feel hungry somewhere around 12.30pm at the latest. This has nothing to do with how much you had to eat for breakfast – it is your body's inner clock working and informing you that lunchtime is approaching. Similarly, if you always go to bed at 11pm, your mind and body will prepare to shut down for the night a short while before that. So try and select a regular time to practise self-hypnosis. You will find that your mind soon begins to expect it at that time and will therefore be at its most receptive.

The ideal time for practising self-hypnosis is when you are in bed at night, just before going to sleep. This is because, as illustrated in chapter two, the conscious mind shuts down when you sleep, leaving your subconscious to work on whatever you have fed into it immediately beforehand. If your subconscious is filled with the positive thoughts of self-hypnosis all night long, it will work even harder to turn those thoughts into reality in the days that follow. If just before sleep is not convenient for you, try and find some period of the day or evening when you will not be watching the clock, or anticipating going somewhere or doing something important immediately afterwards – this will make deep relaxation difficult and render the whole process less effective.

Choose a suitable place

You need to be as comfortable as possible. If you are practising the technique just before going to sleep, you can lie in bed. But whatever the time of day, these are the things that matter:

- Be comfortable. Whether on a chair or bed, make sure that the cushions are adjusted to suit you and that your head and neck are supported. A low-backed chair may cause you discomfort in your neck when you relax. Don't wear any tight-fitting garments – take off your shoes, release any buttons or buckles that might not be comfortable if you are sitting in a relaxed position for twenty minutes or so.
- Adjust the temperature if necessary. You need to be warm but not too hot, so you might want to close a window or cover yourself with a light blanket. If you feel cold, your muscles will automatically become more tense, and this is exactly what we are trying to avoid.
- Avoid noise. Turn off the television, hi-fi or radio. Take the telephone receiver off the hook, turn on the answer machine or arrange for someone else to deal with phone calls. There may be noises from the outside world but these will not bother you once you begin to relax.
- Be alone. It is extremely difficult to relax fully when someone else is in the room, as part of you will be aware that you are being watched. The exceptions to that are if you happen to be with a professional hypnotherapist, who will be quite used to the process, or if you have chosen to ask someone you trust to read the script for you. But if there are other people in the house, ask them not to disturb you until you have finished your period of self-hypnosis (which is unlikely to last more than 20-30 minutes at the most).

PHYSICAL RELAXATION

Now for the relaxation process itself. The first stage of this is the physical relaxation of your body – a process not unlike the early stages of yoga. Beginning with your feet and working upward through the body, first tense then relax each set of muscles in turn. The more you tense your muscles, the more fully they relax afterwards. Remember to concentrate on those muscles around your shoulders, neck, jaw and face, as it is here that stress and tension tends to accumulate.

One important point to remember is that if any parts of your body are in pain or would become painful if tension was increased, then please do not do so. Causing or increasing pain will hardly lead to deep relaxation. In such cases, when you reach that particular part of your body, simply imagine it becoming warm and relaxed and that will be sufficient for the purpose.

Breathing
Once you have become aware of a relaxed feeling in your physical body, it is time to concentrate on your breathing. Take a few moments to become aware of the rhythm of your breathing as it is now – and then see if you can slow it down a little. Although in general it is important to be able to breathe deeply from the diaphragm, rather than from the upper chest (as most of us do most of the time), it is not what we are concentrating on for the purpose of self-hypnosis. What you are trying to achieve and maintain is a slow, regular rhythm. If this is new to you and you are experiencing any difficulty, it can be helpful to count in your head 'one' each time you breathe in and 'two' each time you breathe out.

Become heavy
Starting once again with your feet and working upwards through your body, try to imagine each area in turn becoming very, very heavy. Of course, you may know you are able to get up and walk around should you want to, but try to imagine that your body and limbs feel so heavy that it would be too much effort for you even

to try to do so. Once you have reached that stage of heaviness, you have completed the actual induction technique, which is the first part of any session of self-hypnosis.

Slow down
If you are practising this technique using your thought processes rather than a cassette recording, you will probably go through each stage at a slower and slower pace, as you become more relaxed. If you are preparing a cassette in advance, however, remember to speak much more slowly than you would in normal conversation.

As your conscious mind relaxes and the subconscious mind comes to the fore, spoken words are absorbed ever more slowly. In fact, as I tell those people I am training to become professional hypnotherapists, speak really slowly – and then slow down. It is impossible to speak too slowly at this point, but it is certainly possible to speak too quickly for the subconscious to take in all that is being said.

Barriers to effective relaxation
There are some things that could make relaxation difficult in the initial stages, particularly for those people who are new to the technique.
- Try to avoid being too analytical of the process. Don't worry about what is happening and why. Questioning is natural and healthy but please look for answers before or after attempting to relax deeply – not while you are doing so. Just put the 'hows' and 'whys' to one side and enjoy the process.
- Don't be afraid to move. As you become more relaxed and experience that heavy feeling, the body's tendency to move at all will be greatly reduced. But if you need to shift position a little to make yourself more comfortable, nothing will go wrong. I have known patients who have been afraid to cough or to scratch an itch on their nose in case they 'break the spell' in some way – but this won't happen. You are far more likely to become tense again by trying to resist the urge to cough than you are by clearing your throat. These things will spoil what

you are doing or prevent its success – unless you allow your concerns to cause you to become tense again.

• Don't allow yourself to become anxious about whether you would cope should an emergency arise. You may be relaxed but you are still aware and in control. So, should there be any need for you to arouse yourself out of the relaxed state and deal with an urgent situation, you will be quite able to do so.

One of my patients, who had a baby of just a few months' old, used to bring the child with her when she came for her appointments. Having fed him just before setting out, she would put him, fast asleep, in his buggy in the corner of the room while she had her therapy. As it happened, the little boy never did wake up while she was with me but, if he had, she would have come out of hypnosis immediately because her mind would have known that it was far more important for her to tend to her child.

The first stage

The relaxation/induction technique you have just been learning about is the essential first stage to any session of self-hypnosis. So, if you are going to use a cassette, I suggest you use a 90-minute tape – 45 minutes each side. Record the script given at the end of the chapter on the first half of each side, leaving the rest blank, ready to be filled by the therapy part of your self-hypnosis. If you speak at the appropriate speed, the script should take about ten minutes to record.

Once you have recorded it (or have found someone who is willing to read it to you), I suggest you practise just that relaxation technique for a week or so before even beginning to create your therapy script. I know it is tempting to go on to the next stage as quickly as possible, but you will obtain greater benefit if you become really adept at relaxing first.

Deepening techniques

Some people have a great deal of stress in their lives, while others have lived with the feelings of stress and tension for so long that they find it hard to put them to one side. If this applies to you, you might find you need what is called a 'deepening technique' before you are able to relax fully. This is simply an extra stage to add on to the relaxation process you have already learned, and it will take you deeper and deeper into the realms of relaxation.

There are several different deepening techniques. If you feel you would benefit from using one of them, select the one that appeals to you the most, then record it after your basic relaxation technique and before going on to the therapy part, which will help you to deal with your own particular problem. Here are a few examples:

- Imagine you are standing in a lift, which is at one of the highest floors of a very tall building – floor 23, for example. As this lift begins to descend, very slowly, to the ground floor, you watch the light on the panel indicating each level – 23, 22, 21… Remember to really 'see' this panel in your mind – don't just count the numbers in your head.

- Lift one arm until it is stretched out at shoulder height. Tell yourself that, as you sink deeper into relaxation, your arm will become heavier and will begin to descend until it is by your side once more. As that arm becomes heavy and descends, your relaxation will, in fact, become far deeper.

- Imagine you are lying on a soft white cloud and that the cloud folds gently around you, like a soft duvet on a comfortable bed. Let the cloud carry you gently through the sky, which changes from the brilliant blue of a sunny day to the indigo of dusk. As you visualize your surroundings becoming darker, you will find that your relaxation becomes deeper.

Reminder

Just before we go on to the script you will be using to induce this deep relaxation/trance state, there is one very important reminder. Whether you record it for yourself or ask someone else to do it for you, never, never play this cassette over to yourself while driving or operating machinery. It is very tempting to use the seemingly wasted time of a long car journey to listen to the cassette and remind yourself of the relaxation process but it would be a very dangerous thing to do. Whether you are using your own cassette or any other hypnosis, relaxation or yoga tape, it will have the effect of lowering your blood pressure and reducing your heart and pulse rate. This is excellent, but not at times when you want to be in a state of high alertness and vigilance. Although you would not actually fall asleep at the wheel, your relaxed state will mean your reactions will be slower. You might not be as aware of what is going on around you and be unable to avoid a potentially dangerous situation quickly enough to prevent an accident. So, for your own safety, only listen to the cassette at a time when you are sitting or lying safely in your chosen place.

THE RELAXATION SCRIPT

Here is the basic induction and relaxation script that will form the preliminary to any hypnotic suggestions you may wish to use to help to overcome the problem you have decided to deal with. Remember to *s p e a k s l o w l y.*

As I sit or lie comfortably in my chosen place, I make sure that my head and neck are well supported, that my legs are not crossed and that my hands are resting, unmoving, in my lap or by my sides. I close my eyes, take one or two deep breaths and begin.

I am going to tense and relax each set of muscles, remembering that, should I be suffering from any aches or pains in my body, I shall refrain from using tension in this area but will simply imagine that it is growing steadily warmer.

First my feet. I tense the muscles in my feet as tightly as I possibly can. Then, after holding that tension for a few moments, I relax my feet as completely as I can. Now I do the same with my legs and my thighs – tensing them and, after a pause, letting them go.

Now I do exactly the same thing with my hands, clenching my fists as I tense the muscles of my hands, waiting, and then relaxing them, allowing my fingers to uncurl and my hands to rest idly once more.

Now I repeat the process with my arms, feeling the muscles tighten, then relax.

Next I concentrate on the whole trunk of my body, from the base of my spine, up through my abdomen, my midriff and my chest until the tension reaches my shoulders. I hold that tension for a moment or two, then all at once let it go so that my body sags and is totally relaxed.

Then I come to the area of greatest tension, the parts of my body where the accumulation of stress is felt more acutely than anywhere else – my shoulders, my neck, my jaw and my face. I tense these areas as much as I can, feeling my jaw tighten, my teeth clench, a frown pulling at my forehead and my shoulders rising up towards my ears. Now I release all those muscles – the frown leaves my face, my jaw relaxes and my shoulders relax.

My breathing is very important and I pause now to become aware of the rhythm and regularity of my breathing. In this instance, it is not the depth of my breathing that I am considering but the gentle, regular rhythm of it. Just for a few moments, in my head I count 'one' each time I breathe in and 'two' each time I breathe out.

Now that my breathing is steady and rhythmic, I take ten slow, deep breaths and, with each one, I am aware that my body is relaxing more and more. By the time I reach the tenth breath, I am very relaxed, my limbs feeling warm and heavy.

To deepen this sense of relaxation even more, I will use my imagination – the power of my own mind – to increase the sense of heaviness that is already spreading within me.

Starting once again with my feet, I imagine they are growing heavier and heavier, as if turned to stone on the ends of my legs. Although I know intellectually that I can get up and walk around whenever I wish, I imagine that my feet are now so heavy that it would be too much effort on my part even to try to stand and walk.

Still using my imagination, I allow that feeling of extreme heaviness to creep from my feet, past my ankles, up my legs, past my knees and up my thighs until it reaches my hips – so that my feet and my legs are now very, very heavy.

Now I do the same thing with my hands, imagining that they too are growing heavier and heavier. Then, still using the power of my own mind, I permit that heavy feeling to spread slowly past my wrists, up my forearms, past my elbows and upper arms until it reaches my shoulders – so that now, just like my legs and feet, my hands and arms are very, very heavy.

Next I turn my concentration and my imagination to the whole of my *body. It is already in a relaxed state but, as I imagine my body growing heavier and heavier, that state of relaxation is increased. My body becomes more and more relaxed as I feel that heaviness spreading upwards from my abdomen, past my waist, up through my chest and reaching my shoulders. I become aware that my shoulders are now growing heavier and heavier as I imagine that they are doing so – and that heaviness spreads upwards to the back of my shoulders, the back of my neck, then up and over my head so that even my eyelids and my jaw become very, very heavy.*

I stay in this position for several moments, enjoying the sensation of true relaxation, knowing I am now in the ideal state for my subconscious mind to accept and work on the words that follow.

Hopefully you will notice some difference in the way you feel from the very first time you use this technique – but if not, don't worry. Continue to practise it daily and you should find that, from about day three onward, you begin to become aware of the benefits. If, after using it every day for a week, you are one of the few people who feel you are not deeply relaxed, then add to it whichever of the described deepening techniques you feel most drawn to. Once you have created a cassette that helps you to relax well and deeply, you can go on to work on formulating the self-hypnosis technique that is going to help you overcome your own particular problem.

AFFIRMATIONS

Affirmations are simply statements that you can read or repeat to yourself over and over to help reinforce the self-hypnosis you have been practising. Although not really sufficient in themselves to bring about the changes you want, they have often proved to be extremely effective as a back-up. Each individual affirmation need consist of no more than a single sentence, which you repeat to yourself, either verbally or mentally, frequently throughout the day. The most important thing about the sentence is that it should assume you have already achieved whatever it is you are setting out to achieve. In other words:

- 'I am happy to take a journey in an aeroplane', not 'I am getting better at making flights.'
- 'I am now a non-smoker' rather than 'I smoke fewer cigarettes than I used to.'
- 'My head feels clear and free from tension', not 'I get fewer headaches than before.'

In chapter one we looked at how important the repetition of words and phrases can be, how advertisers rely on them to persuade us of the benefits of their products, and how we can reinforce weaknesses within ourselves each time we remind ourselves of them. The reverse is also true. Let your mind absorb the positive words and thoughts of your affirmations, and your brain will come to accept those words and thoughts as the truth. There are various ways in which you can use your affirmations once you have created them:

- Simply repeat them over and over to yourself at regular intervals throughout the day.
- Write each one on a small piece of card. Carry these cards with you at all times in a pocket, a briefcase or a handbag. Whenever you have a spare moment, take out one or more of the cards and read it to yourself.
- Write each affirmation on a Post-it note, which you can stick up anywhere and remove without leaving damaging marks. Place these notes on your walls, mirror, doors, fridge – anywhere you have to pass frequently throughout the day. The interesting thing is that you do not even have to stop and make a deliberate effort to read and digest what is on the note – your brain will do that automatically. It is rather like hearing the words of the current number-one song on the radio; you may not intend to learn these words, but hear them often enough and sooner or later you will know them by heart.

Case study: Gemma

When Gemma was studying for her A levels she was beset by nervousness. She knew she had done her revision and was quite capable of answering any questions she might be asked. She was a bright girl, who had always been a good and conscientious student, but in the past she had let herself down more than once when it came to exams because of nerves. Fear of failure would make her so tense and anxious that she often wasted precious minutes during the exams themselves by being so rigid with tension, she could neither think nor write. Because her chances of going to the university of her choice depended on the results she obtained in her A levels, Gemma was beginning to panic as the exams drew nearer.

Then she heard about self-hypnosis, which is extremely effective when dealing with nervousness of any sort. Not only that but she was told of the value of affirmations. She decided to stick up yellow Post-it notes around her room – on the mirror she had to look in when brushing her hair, on the desk where she did her studying and her revision, and on the cover she had to pull back in order to go to bed.

There were very few words written on these notes – 'Calm and serene', 'Pass', 'Success', and so on. Wherever Gemma looked, there would be another note bearing a positive word or phrase. Without making any conscious effort to absorb the meaning of these words, they came to rest in Gemma's mind and therefore had the effect of persuading her subconscious that they were true statements. Then all her subconscious had to do was to ensure she lived up to them.

There is an added advantage in using yellow Post-it notes, as it has been shown that psychologically yellow is the colour that most effectively attracts the attention. So without any deliberate effort on Gemma's part, her eyes (and mind) were automatically attracted to them.

As you progress through this book, you will find that, in addition to suggested scripts for overcoming the various problems, there will be a few suggested affirmations for you to use in whichever way you choose. Of course, you can also write extra ones for yourself and let them play their part in helping you to improve your life.

4

Giving Up Smoking

Perhaps one of the most common reasons for someone to seek the help of hypnotherapy is because they wish to stop smoking. But it is also very common for those who know little about hypnosis to think that the therapy is some sort of magic wand that will make this happen, and all they have to do is sit back and wait for the miracle to occur.

Sadly this is not the case. Yes, hypnotherapy is definitely one of the most effective means of helping anyone to give up smoking – but the desire has to come from the smoker. No therapy is going to make you stop smoking if you don't really want to. So the first thing you have to consider is whether you truly want to give up smoking. Before you rush to say that of course you do, stop and think. There is a great difference between wanting to give up and thinking you should. Or between wanting to give up and someone else thinking you should – whether that someone is your partner, your boss or your son or daughter.

Most smokers are perfectly well aware that it would be far better for them in many ways if they were to break the habit. They would run less risk of permanently – even fatally – damaging their health, they would have more money to spend on other things, and their senses of smell and taste would improve. But even being fully aware of all these things does not necessarily make the individual want to give up, any more than knowing the calories contained in a bar of chocolate can make the overweight person want to stop eating it.

If someone comes to consult me for hypnotherapy in order to

give up smoking but cannot tell me in all honesty that they really want to stop, I will not take them on as a patient. It would be a waste of my time and their money – and it wouldn't work. That doesn't mean that the door is being shut permanently on the possibility of that person becoming a non-smoker but it does mean that this might not be the right time.

There are also those people who believe they would just like to cut down on the amount they smoke. Perhaps they will just smoke at weekends, or maybe they will just allow themselves a cigarette after meals. I can tell you now that this doesn't work. Anyone who decides to smoke less as opposed to giving up altogether will soon find an excuse to smoke more again. Until you can come to terms with the fact that giving up smoking means stopping for ever, you might as well not bother trying to kick the habit.

Let's suppose you have thought long and hard about whether or not you want to stop smoking and stop forever. You have come to the conclusion that you definitely want to give up the habit, knowing you can never smoke again – where do you go from here?

There are, of course, other suggested methods for giving up smoking. You could try 'cold turkey' – just telling yourself you have had your last cigarette and determine not to have another. There are a few – very few – people who can manage this but it is an extremely difficult and stressful way of giving up. If you smoke more than a very small number of cigarettes (or cigars or pipes of tobacco) a day, you are already addicted to nicotine and so giving up just like that is going to create withdrawal symptoms. These can be uncomfortable for you and – depending on how they affect you – difficult for those around you.

You could try cutting down a few at a time but it is astonishing how easy it is for us to fool ourselves. You conveniently 'forget' the cigarette offered and accepted at lunchtime. You have a bad day and decide it won't hurt to have an extra one to calm the nerves just this once. You go to a social function and stand with a drink in one hand and cigarette in the other because this is what one does at this sort of function. There are all sorts of patches, pills and chewing gum available, each of which is designed to help you cut down on your smoking – and to a certain extent they do. The trouble is, they all contain nicotine so they do nothing to decrease your addiction. You either become addicted to the cure or, when you stop using it, the craving for nicotine makes you go back to smoking once again.

Let's suppose you have reached the stage where you have decided you definitely want to give up smoking and that self-hypnosis is the method you have chosen. Now you need to consider why it is you want to stop. There may be all sorts of reasons:

• *Bad for your health.* This has been proven to be true. Of course, there is always someone who had a grandfather who smoked 60 cigarettes a day all his life and still lived to be 96 – but then there are also individuals who manage to survive dreadful disasters such as explosions, volcanoes, train crashes, and so on. You can be sure that, for every 96-year-old grandfather, there have been thousands of people who have become seriously ill and even died for no other reason than that they smoked too much for too long.

Most people who think about smoking's adverse effects on health think primarily about lung cancer. And it is true that thousands of people worldwide die each year because of lung cancer contracted solely as a result of their smoking. But your health can be affected in other ways too. Apart from making strokes and heart attacks more likely, there is the dreadful disease of emphysema – when the air sacs of the lungs are damaged, causing breathlessness. You may not die as quickly, but you won't get much pleasure from your life.

When I was a small child I had a great-uncle that suffered from emphysema. This man had smoked about sixty cigarettes a day for most of his working life – but remember this was at a time when such a thing was considered normal for a working man, as smoking was not looked down upon in the way it is now. For the last ten years of his life my great-uncle could not take a deep breath. Walking from one side of the room to the other exhausted him – his face would go grey and he would gasp for air. He became a prisoner in his own home, making my great-aunt a prisoner at the same time.

Being no more than six or seven years old at the time, I did not understand what the problem was. All I knew was that I was terrified of this man whose face was always a funny colour, whose shoulders were permanently somewhere around the level of his ears as he fought for each breath, and who made such peculiar wheezing noises. It was a very long time ago but the picture of my great-uncle remains with me still, although now I can look back on him with sympathy.

- *Money.* Strangely enough, money is very rarely the most important reason for someone wanting to stop smoking. Even bearing in mind the frightening cost of tobacco products today, most people who really want to smoke somehow find the money to do so. Of course, it is an additional benefit when they do give up to find that they can perhaps take the family on a good holiday with the cash they save.
- *Social acceptance.* Of all the reasons for giving up, this is comparatively recent. Over the past few years, smoking has become less and less acceptable in both public and private places. At one time there would be small corner of a restaurant designated for non-smokers; now it is the smokers who are pushed into the corner or, in many eating places, not allowed to smoke at all. Trains, aeroplanes, office premises, theatres, cinemas, shops and many other places either permit very limited smoking or none at all. People who at one time would hesitate to reply in the negative to the question, 'Do you mind if I smoke?' now do not hesitate to make their views clear. Many a smoker has had to spend time shivering in a cold garden because their host does not like people to smoke in the house. So wherever you go, you are made to feel the outcast and, if you are someone who really has trouble in going without a cigarette for any length of time, you may find it extremely difficult to cope with a visit to the theatre or a long journey by public transport.
- *The smell.* This is something ex-smokers become aware of quite soon after quitting – and something that those who have never smoked have been all too aware of for a long, long time. Go to

any gathering where there are smokers and your clothes – right down to your underwear – smell of stale tobacco. Even worse, your hair smells of it too. But if you are the smoker, you also have to face the fact that your skin and your breath smell like an old ashtray – not a very pleasant thought.

While someone is a smoker, they are often unaware of these smells. I have even had a patient turn up for a second appointment assuring me that he had not touched a cigarette since our last meeting, when the smell of his breath was enough to tell me he had smoked within the last hour. Another patient told me he had to give up as he was smoking without his partner realizing it. He obviously did not realize that all the peppermints in the world couldn't hide from someone close to you the fact that you are a smoker.

TWO STAGES

Some people are so ready to end the cycle of self-abuse that is smoking that they can begin straight away. Others find they need to make a commitment with themselves by setting a date on which they will give up smoking forever – perhaps the next Monday or the first day of the following month. This is not the same as giving themselves a licence to smoke twice as much as usual in the intervening period, but a way of giving themselves the opportunity to consolidate in their own mind what they are doing and, more importantly, why.

If you fall into the latter category then stop now for a moment and make a decision about the date on which you are going to become a non-smoker. Don't make it too far ahead or you will always find a reason for postponing it. About a week is an ideal time, so you could tell yourself that, one week from today, you will stop smoking forever.

Once you have told yourself that fact, take every opportunity in the coming seven days to tell everyone else that this is what you intend to do. Every time you tell someone, you are reinforcing the words in your own mind and making them into fact instead of just thought. Hopefully you won't have any so-called 'friends' who think it is a great idea to try and tempt those giving up smoking to fall by the wayside and smoke again. If you know such people, you will also know they are not your friends. Friends want you to succeed. Those who try to put temptation in your way are usually those who have tried to give up smoking themselves and have failed. They don't like to feel inferior, so they make sure that as many other people as possible fail as well. All we can do is pity them – and steer clear of them.

During the days before you actually give up, see if you can discover what the trigger is for you. What is it that, in the past, has made you reach automatically for a cigarette? Once you know what it is, you can go out of your way to ensure you realize when such a trigger is approaching so that you are in a position to counteract it.

For one person the trigger might be the telephone ringing. Without thinking, they will light up a cigarette before answering that phone. Another will automatically smoke on social occasions, particularly when alcohol is involved. Yet another will smoke to 'calm the nerves' at times of great anxiety or stress. Once you realize your own trigger, you can prepare to find another way of dealing with the situation.

Another thing to consider while waiting for stop-smoking day to arrive is that, with the knowledge we now have about the effects of smoking on health, it is a form of self-abuse. I am sure you do not want to be among those people, so deserving of our pity, who find ways of abusing themselves. And do you really want to think you have so lost control of your life that you are dependent upon something as ridiculous as a few dried-up leaves rolled in a piece of paper?

So, for those of you who feel it would be easier to make a commitment to give up smoking on a specifically named day in the near future, here is a self-hypnosis script to be used in the meantime. As usual, it follows on from the induction and relaxation script you have already recorded:

I have come to one of the most important decisions of my life. I have decided to stop smoking, to become a non-smoker forever. It doesn't matter how long I have been smoking, it doesn't matter why I began in the first place, and it doesn't matter whether I have tried to give up in the past. All that matters is that I have made a promise to myself that on (insert chosen day) I shall become a non-smoker.

As that day approaches, I become more excited about what I am about to achieve. I am going to change my life forever and, in doing so, I shall boost my self-esteem and my belief in myself. I shall be accomplishing something I really want to do and, in doing so, I shall be taking control of my own life. I shall prove to myself and others that I am my own person, not someone who is a slave to a trigger or a habit. I intend to choose what I take into my body and I choose not to absorb anything that I know is capable of doing me great harm.

I have thought about the situations that have, in the past, triggered in me a need for a cigarette and I am prepared to face them in the following way.

As I relax now, I concentrate on my right hand and I place the tips of the thumb and first finger of that hand together. Now I do the same with my left hand. Gently but firmly I press the tips of each hand together three times – press and release, press and release, press and release. Now I relax my hands completely again.

What I have just done by that simple action is to fix in my subconscious the link between that gentle pressure and the feeling of deep relaxation. Whenever a former trigger moment arrives in the future, all I have to do is to put together my thumb and finger tips, and press and release three times, and I shall feel so relaxed that I will have no need of any artificial substance. I am stronger and more powerful than any trigger moment that might arise.

Now, as I relax even more deeply, I contemplate the pleasure of being able to take deep, deep breaths of clean, fresh air once I am a non-smoker. In preparation for that time, I practise breathing deeply now. Making sure that I breathe right from the diaphragm, I take several deep breaths in… and out, in… and out, in… and out.

I think of all the pleasures of being a non-smoker – of improving my health, sparing those around me from having to breathe in stale tobacco, feeling clean and free from unpleasant odours, and of being truly proud of myself for taking control of my own life. Those things seem so *wonderful to me that I cannot wait for them to be mine and I look forward in keen anticipation to (insert day) when I shall become a non-smoker.*

I would suggest you use that particular cassette twice a day for the week before you give up smoking so that by the time the actual date arrives, you will be really anxious for it to be here, bringing with it all those benefits you have considered.

Helpful affirmations
- I can't wait for next (insert day) when I become a non-smoker.
- I now have the tools to combat any former trigger moments.
- I have taken the first step towards being in control of my own life.

Fixing
You will have noticed that built into that script is a small physical movement you can make that will immediately make your subconscious recall the sensation of relaxation. This is known as 'fixing' or 'anchoring' and can be very effective. It doesn't matter where you are or what you are doing, if a trigger moment arrives all you have to do is put the tips of the thumbs and first fingers of each hand together, then press and release them three times, and the moment will pass without problem. It will have lost its power over you.

This way of fixing doesn't just apply to smoking. Whatever your current problem, if there is any time when you begin to feel uneasy, you just have to perform that very small movement – and it is quite possible to do it without anyone else noticing – and you will feel stronger, more relaxed and more in charge of yourself and your reactions.

THE THREE REASONS FOR SMOKING

There are three main reasons why people smoke, even though they really might not want to. They are:
- Desire

- Habit
- Addiction

Desire

The desire to smoke is the easiest one to overcome by means of self-hypnosis, because the basis is already within you. The very fact you are trying to give up means that the desire is already there, even if it is a little weak. Making the commitment with yourself and using the first script in the intervening period should be sufficient to rid yourself of the desire completely. In fact, most people, by the time they have used the first script three or four times, cannot wait to reach 'non-smoking day' and put their plans into action.

Habit

This is partly dealt with and overcome by means of recognizing the trigger moments, and dealing with them using the fixing technique. The other types of habit – when perhaps someone offers you a cigarette and, because you have always done so, you reach out and take one before you have had time to realize what you are doing – will be dealt with effectively by the second script; the one you will start to use when your chosen day arrives.

Addiction

Depending upon how many cigarettes you smoke each day, and how long you have been a smoker, you will be addicted to nicotine to a greater or lesser degree. This is not something that will disappear overnight, but you will now have the tool to combat it and to support yourself until that addiction leaves you. You will have your second script.

In most cases of self-hypnosis, it is sufficient for the script to be read, or the cassette to be played, once a day. When dealing with smoking, I usually suggest that this is done at least twice a day – and more, if you feel you need it. Working through the script and reinforcing your subconscious desire to be a non-smoker will help to deal with the problem of nicotine addiction and it will hardly trouble you at all.

BARRIERS TO STOPPING SMOKING

We humans are contrary beings and it is quite common for us, however much we want to improve our lives in a particular way, to think up all sorts of reasons why we should not do so. Rather than try to suppress these barriers, perhaps it is better to look at them and examine their validity.

Gaining weight
One of the commonest excuses you will hear people give in order to escape the need to stop smoking is that they don't want to put on weight – and they think this will be inevitable. This is just not true. Let's look at what happens.

It is a fact that, in the first five or six weeks after giving up smoking, most people will put on a few pounds in weight. This is because of an alteration in the fluid content in their body. But, provided you are not eating any more than you did before, after that five or six weeks the excess weight will disappear as your body adjusts itself to the new regime.

Of course, if you substitute sweets, biscuits or nuts for cigarettes then you will put on weight – anyone would. And the only reason for doing this is usually that the former smoker is so used to transferring something from hand to mouth that, deprived of his paper full of leaves, he turns to something to eat instead. So plan to do something else with your hands instead or, if you must have something in your mouth, try ordinary chewing gum – not the most elegant of habits but it might help you over the first couple of weeks.

Damaged health
'I've been smoking for so long, the harm has probably already been done.' I have heard this from many a would-be non-smoker. Whether any harm has already been done can be ascertained by a check-up with your general practitioner. If it has then the sooner you stop smoking and start repairing as much of the damage as possible, the better.

If your doctor gives you the good news that you have managed to avoid any permanent damage to your health so far, you can be reassured that, once you have stopped smoking and the nicotine has had time to clear from your system, you are no more or less likely to develop a smoking-related illness than someone who has never smoked.

Other people around me are smokers
It is true that, if you are surrounded by smokers, it may at first be harder to stop smoking yourself. But, if you persevere, once you have stopped, the fact that your colleagues, your friends or your partner are still smokers will actually reinforce your determination not to go back to the habit. What tends to happen is that you begin to feel pity for those who are still slaves to the foul-smelling dried leaves and who still go around smelling of old ashtrays.

READY TO BEGIN

The day has arrived. The date you selected as the one on which you are to become a non-smoker. And it is going to be much easier than you ever imagined because you will have your script to help you. Use it daily – more than once a day if you feel the need.

But first – and this is very important – seek out any smoking paraphernalia you may have in the house or at work. Cigarettes, tobacco, ashtrays, matches, lighters – get them together and throw the lot in the dustbin. If you feel you can't do this, you need to work further on your first cassette, perhaps setting a new date for a few days' time. After all, if you are to become a non-smoker from today, you will never need any of those items again, will you? And there is the psychological aspect too: should you ever feel tempted to smoke in the future, there is a big difference between taking a cigarette out of a cupboard in your house and deliberately going to a shop to buy some. You are far less likely to do the latter as it would really be letting yourself down and, even if you set out to do so, by the time you reached the shop, your resolve will have returned and you will be able to restrain yourself from making that purchase.

Here is the script that is going to make you a non-smoker. If you are recording it on tape, remember to follow on from the original induction/relaxation exercise.

I have decided to be a non-smoker. The very fact that I am giving up my time to follow this exercise makes it almost inevitable that I will succeed. I know that there are thousands of people going around saying that they wish to stop smoking – but I am making a deliberate commitment of my time and my effort and this makes success most likely.

Because I am now a non-smoker, I am going to become more aware, with each passing day, of an increased sense of well-being. Day by day I am going to feel fitter, healthier and more positive. I will be able to take deeper breaths than before, my energy will be greater as my lungs become clear of the toxins that have been filling them.

I will become increasingly aware of the smell of stale tobacco on other people – on their clothes, their hair, their skin and their breath. I will be grateful that my clothes, hair, skin and breath no longer have this foul smell. I have too much pride in myself to allow myself to smell so dirty.

I have learned to acknowledge the triggers that formerly caused me to reach for a cigarette and, armed with this knowledge, I can prepare myself for what might otherwise have been difficult situations by using the fixing technique with my fingers and thumbs to increase my sense of relaxation – and thereby eliminate my need for tobacco.

Because I am a human being, I accept that, in the immediate future, there may be times when I will forget I am a non-smoker. Perhaps at a party someone will offer me a cigarette and, without thinking and because I have always done so, I will take one, place it in my mouth and light it.

I will imagine I am doing that now, placing a cigarette between my lips and lighting it. Suddenly my mouth is filled with the most revolting taste I have ever experienced. I imagine this foul taste filling my mouth, drying and burning it, and then the black filth spreads down my throat and into my lungs where it spreads its poison until the insides of my lungs are coated with it. I know that this poison can certainly make me ill and could even kill me if I do not get rid of it.

So now, immediately, I imagine that all the foulness has gone from my mouth, my throat and my lungs. I am breathing clean, cool, fresh air. My mouth tastes pleasant again.

Should I ever, at any time in the future, accept a cigarette without thinking about what I am doing, the first taste will immediately bring back to me all that filth and foulness, and I will put the cigarette out at once.

I am so proud of myself for doing something many others are incapable of doing – for taking charge of my own life. I feel happy and proud, and I pity those who are not able to break free from the life-threatening habit of smoking. With each day that passes, I feel stronger and healthier, and I know I am doing all that I can to increase the power of both my body and mind.

I allow another image to come into my mind. I picture a very busy road – perhaps a motorway or a large dual carriageway – on a very hot summer's day. The day is so hot that the surface of the road becomes sticky with the heat. But as soon as the temperature cools, the surface of the road hardens once more – hardens sufficiently for cars, coaches and huge lorries to drive along without leaving any mark.

That road surface is covered with tar – the same substance that I have been allowing into my arteries and my lungs. When it is warm, it is soft and slips down easily. But once it has cooled, like the road surface, it has lined my arteries and my lungs with a substance so hard that huge lorries could drive over it. I choose not to allow such a substance into my body ever again. I choose to keep my arteries and my air passages clear and to allow my lungs to remain pink and healthy.

I am so proud of myself for having taken this step towards increasing not only the length of my life but the health I experience. It makes me happy and excited to proclaim to myself and to the world that I am now a non-smoker.

Just a comment about the foul taste mentioned in that script. If it should happen that you accept a cigarette from anyone without thinking and that you light it, the first taste will indeed be as dreadful as the description and you will be aware of it spreading throughout your body. This is not designed to make you feel ill but just to jog your memory and remind you that you are now a non-smoker so that you put the cigarette out as soon as possible. Should you make the deliberate decision to continue to smoke it, however, the foul taste will disappear and it will taste just as it has always done. So, should the occasion arise, make sure you take the decision to extinguish the cigarette immediately.

Use this second script at least once a day for about a week. After that, how often you use it depends on you. Most people find they don't need it at all after the first week but some feel that it helps to boost their confidence in themselves as non-smokers if they use it every few days for a couple of weeks more. It is entirely up to you. You will know when the time comes that you don't need it any more.

Even after you have been a non-smoker for some time, don't get rid of the script because it is just possible that some emergency might arise in the future.

Case study: Peter
Many years ago, by using the method described in this chapter, Peter became a non-smoker. He had previously been smoking about twenty-five cigarettes a day but stopped completely and even found that, after the first week, he had no more need of the script.

Then, suddenly, about two years later, Peter's father was killed in a road accident. Peter was devastated – he and his father had been extremely close and the suddenness of his death shocked him dreadfully. The uncle who broke the news to him, thinking he was helping Peter to cope with the shock, offered him a cigarette and, without thinking Peter took it. Because of his numbness at the news he had just received, the foul taste was not present and, almost without tasting it at all, he smoked the entire cigarette.

A few days later, I heard from an anxious Peter. He had not smoked another cigarette since that dreadful day but, because he was feeling so low, he was afraid he might do so. I suggested that he went back to using the script that had helped him in the first place and that was in fact all he needed. He telephoned me a few weeks later to say that he was still – and would remain – a non-smoker.

5

Losing Weight

A part from wanting to give up smoking, the desire to lose weight used to be the most common reason for someone to visit a hypnotherapist. Over the years, as people have felt more able to talk about their emotions, their stresses and what has happened to them in the past, the number and variety of other presenting problems has increased. In spite of this, however, a considerable number of people still choose hypnotherapy as a means of helping to rid themselves of excess weight.

While discussing weight and the associated problems that might arise, I would like to mention severe eating disorders such as anorexia or bulimia nervosa. These conditions are not appropriate to treat using self-hypnosis. Because they are extremely serious and can have life-threatening consequences, and because they normally arise when the sufferer has a very low opinion of themselves, anyone suffering from such a condition really must consult a professional for help. There have been many occasions when I have worked with anorexics or bulimics and helped them on the way to recovery, but this has always been with the consent of their doctor or consultant.

Even setting aside such severe conditions as anorexia and bulimia, there are some people whose weight gain has come about because of an emotional problem.

Case study: Kathy

Kathy came to see me because she wanted to lose weight. Over a period of about two years she had put on three stone and she was anxious to lose it and get back to her normal size. Although she proved to be an excellent subject for hypnosis and was willing to co-operate with me in every way, Kathy did not seem to respond to the usual weight loss technique. After two unsuccessful sessions, I decided to try and find out if there was something more serious behind Kathy's steady weight gain – something more than just eating or drinking too much.

Sometimes someone (more usually a woman, although occasionally it can be a man) either has such low self-esteem or is so guilty about something, or so angry with themselves, that the subconscious collects and maintains the excess weight as a form of punishment. When I put this to Kathy, she recognized herself straight away and told me her story.

A few years earlier, when she was in her early 20s, Kathy had begun an affair with a man who worked in the same office as she did. Both she and this man were married to other people but they continued with the affair nonetheless, although neither of them was what you would call promiscuous by nature. Eventually, because they each felt guilty about cheating on their respective partners, they came to the conclusion that the affair must come to an end. The man left the company – and indeed the district – and Kathy never saw him again.

Fortunately for both marriages, neither of their partners had ever discovered the infidelity and Kathy had made the decision not to tell her husband for fear of destroying the relationship. Perhaps because of her feelings of guilt, or perhaps it was because of the stress of keeping that secret to herself, Kathy began subconsciously to punish herself by putting on a considerable amount of weight. Three stones of excess weight is quite a lot for anyone, but particularly for someone like Kathy, who was naturally slender and small-boned.

When we discussed the situation, Kathy agreed that she still felt guilty (although she had never been tempted to have another affair). She also added that at least the excess weight would make her so unattractive to men that no one would want to have a relationship with her in the future, so she was unlikely to be confronted by temptation. Ironically, the excess weight did not have the effect of making Kathy unattractive because her vivacity and pleasant nature still shone through – but she did not realize this and now considered herself the dowdy and fat women she felt she deserved to be.

We did go on to work on this problem and eventually Kathy lost all her excess weight – but the methods were different to those used when dealing with overweight due to eating more than is right for the individual's basic shape and metabolism. You will find information on how to create a script for problems such as Kathy's later in this book. What we are going to deal with in this chapter is what I will call 'ordinary' excess weight. That is, when someone weighs more than they would like to, or more than is healthy for their height and frame, and wishes to lose weight.

NO DIET!

The first thing to realize is that there is no actual diet involved in this process. No food is forbidden. There are various reasons for this:
- Suppose you are told you can eat anything you like except, say, biscuits. What happens the first time you have a terrible day, when everything seems to go wrong, or when it rains for days on end, or when your partner leaves you for another – or any other occurrence that makes you feel miserable? We all have days like that. If you have been told that you can eat anything in the world except biscuits, the first thing you are going to want on such a day is a biscuit. You feel deprived, you feel fed up, you don't care about yourself or anything else – and you feel that everyone else is allowed to eat biscuits, so why shouldn't you? If, on the other hand, biscuits are allowed anyway, there is no need to have a craving for them on one of those bad days.

- If ordinary diets – whether counting points, cutting calories, high-protein, low-fat or anything else – really worked, everyone would be slim. The trouble with all those diets is that they make you think of food all the time. If you are counting calories and are allowed, say, 1200 calories a day, you might feel quite full one day after using up only 1000 of those calories, but you still find yourself looking around for something that will make up the other 200 – the ones 'owed to you'. On the other hand, there might come a day when you have used up far more physical energy and you really feel the need for extra food. If that extra takes you over your allotted 1200 calories, you will feel guilty that you have ruined your diet.
- If you stick to a diet and manage to lose weight by cutting out carbohydrates or fats or chocolate, what happens as soon as you have reached your desired weight? Human nature will decree that you deserve to be able to eat all those hitherto forbidden foods, and all that weight, so painstakingly lost, will soon pile on again. If you have not deprived yourself of any particular food while losing weight, there is nothing to go back to once you have reached your target weight – so no weight gain ensues.

WHAT DOES SELF-HYPNOSIS ACHIEVE?

If you are not going on a diet, how is self-hypnosis going to help you lose weight? The answer is that self-hypnosis is going to help you to have a greatly reduced appetite. If your appetite is less, then, whatever you eat, you will not be able to eat as much of it. If you eat less, you must lose weight.

THE RULES

There are only three basic rules that you have to bear in mind while losing weight by self-hypnosis. They are very simple but also very important – and the key to the success of the whole process.

1. Weigh yourself only once a week

I told you the rules were simple and this one certainly is – and yet the natural temptation for anyone trying to lose weight is to hop on the bathroom scales daily (or even twice a day) to see how things are going. But I can assure you that this can lead to disaster and failure. For most people – and women in particular – the fluid content of the body fluctuates daily. If you weigh yourself every day and suddenly see that you appear to have gained a pound, you might become disheartened and give the whole thing up – when all that has happened is that your fluid level is up a bit that day. Conversely, if you seem to have lost quite a lot of weight between one day and the next, you might become over-confident and careless, just because your fluid level happens to be quite low. Similarly, if (surely not!) you have cheated and eaten more than you should, yet the scales do not show you have gained weight, you might be tempted to try and get away with it more often. While if you know you have obeyed the rules and yet – horror of horrors! – the scales show an increase in weight, you could feel like giving the whole thing up as a bad job. So weigh yourself just once a week please, preferably at the same time of day and wearing the same type of clothes, and you are far more likely to get a fair and accurate reading of your weight loss for the week.

2. If you are hungry, you must eat

There is no need to go around with that dreadful hollow feeling in your stomach, even if it makes you feel pious, because you know how hungry you are and yet you still manage to deprive yourself of food. Not only are you likely to give in and reach for the nearest (and often most fattening) food around but you could be harming your health. Built into the self-hypnosis programme for reducing your appetite is the fact that when your body needs food for nutritional reasons, you will feel hungry. It is essential, therefore, that you acknowledge that hunger (which is not at all the same thing as desiring food for its own sake) and have something to eat.

3. If you are not hungry, you must not eat anything at all

It doesn't matter that the clock has just chimed one and you always have your lunch at one o'clock. It doesn't matter whether it is one hour or six hours since you last ate. If you cannot say with absolute honesty that you feel hungry, you must not eat any food at all. This doesn't have to be as anti-social as it sounds. There is nothing to stop you sitting down with others who are eating; there is nothing to stop you having a drink while you sit with them. The only thing you must not do is eat anything yourself.

As previously mentioned, one of the reasons most diets fail is because of the feeling of being deprived of the foods you most enjoy. But you are not being deprived of any food – you are simply being asked to adjust the time at which you eat it. If you have just prepared a meal you would normally enjoy but you know you are not hungry, you don't have to deprive yourself of that meal – just wait a little longer before eating it. When you feel hungry, eat that meal and enjoy every mouthful.

There is a simple trick that might help you to control the amount you eat – particularly if you are someone who has always been in the habit of finishing whatever is on your plate (some of our mothers have a great deal to answer for!) When you are hungry and about to enjoy your food, put onto your plate half the amount you would normally expect to serve yourself. Eat it and enjoy it, then wait for ten minutes. If you can still say honestly that you are hungry, serve and eat the rest. But if you are no longer hungry (and remember self-hypnosis will reduce your appetite), then put it to one side and have it later.

We all have in our brain a sort of nutritional thermostat, which tells us when we have had enough to eat. But, particularly in the comparatively affluent western world, most of us don't stop eating when that point it reached. Very few of us ever feel hungry. We eat because we enjoy it, because other people are eating or because, according to the clock, it is eating time. Even when we want to listen to this nutritional thermostat, by the time it clicks into action, we have usually eaten something more. But if you pause for about ten minutes, you will be able to tell whether or not you are truly hungry or whether that extra food should be saved for later.

The one thing you should not try to cut down is drinking. Fluids are essential for the efficient working of the body and you could do yourself harm if you reduce them drastically. It is true that an excessive intake of fluid on one day might cause the scales to register more the following day, but this is something the body will adjust naturally – and remember, you are only going to weigh yourself once a week so this won't be a problem for you.

Within reason, have your normal drink – fruit juice, water, tea, coffee, or whatever – whenever you fancy. Although nothing is forbidden, there are a couple of points to bear in mind. One is that alcohol is likely to affect you far more if you are eating considerably less, so do be careful not to overdo your alcoholic intake. The other is that sweet, fizzy drinks can often supply an excess of calories for little or no nutritional value, so if possible try to keep to low-calorie soft drinks.

Those three rules, and the fact you will be reducing your appetite by means of self-hypnosis, form the basis for this weight-loss plan. If you adhere strictly to the rules and use your script regularly – and provided you do not have any physical condition that dramatically affects your metabolism – you cannot fail to lose weight. It is impossible to say at what rate you will lose weight because this will vary from person to person – indeed for one individual it can vary from week to week. But this does not matter. In fact, doctors have now proved that gradual weight loss is more effective than rapid and extreme weight loss.

VISUALIZATION

The other very important aspect of weight loss that will be incorporated in your script is visualization. You are going to learn to picture yourself looking exactly as you really want to look; seeing yourself as the shape and size you really wish to be. This is actually far more important than worrying about what the bathroom scales register. It doesn't really matter what you weigh, provided you know you look and feel right. And some of the charts available are quite unrealistic and give desired weights, which would be unachievable – and sometimes quite unhealthy – for many people. The trick with this sort of visualization is that you 'see' in your mind the finished result. If you concentrate on just being a bit slimmer than you are now, when you reach that stage your subconscious will be satisfied and you are likely to stop losing weight. So however distant that target may appear to be, make sure your visualization shows what you consider to be the 'ideal' you.

If you are ready to begin losing weight once and for all, here is your script. Again, whether you are learning or recording this, it should always follow on from the initial induction technique you learned at the start.

I have decided to lose my excess weight and I know that, using the wonderful method of self-hypnosis, I am going to achieve my aim. Not only will I lose any surplus weight I have been carrying around, because I am not depriving myself of anything at all, I will not put it all on again afterwards.

I am going to begin by using my imagination. I am going to imagine that I have just eaten a really good and satisfying meal – perhaps a Christmas dinner; perhaps a traditional Sunday lunch. As I relax here now, I can remember such a meal – one that left me feeling satisfied and full, but not at all unwell or uncomfortable.

From this moment onward, that feeling of fullness and satisfaction is going to remain with me almost all the time. The only time it will disappear and leave me feeling hungry is when my body is telling me that I need food for my health's sake.

At this point I am going to remind myself of those three, very important rules – the ones that will ensure this weight-loss technique is a success.

I imagine before me a huge sheet of white paper. On it I see the following instructions being written in large, black capital letters, one letter at a time:

RULE 1: FOR THE REASONS EXPLAINED, I WILL WEIGH

MYSELF ONCE A WEEK ONLY.
RULE 2: IF I AM HUNGRY, I MUST EAT.
RULE 3: IF I AM NOT HUNGRY, I MAY NOT EAT ANYTHING
AT ALL, WHATEVER THE TIME OF DAY OR EVENING.
Those three rules, coupled with the fact I am feeling pleasantly full most of the time, will ensure that I lose my excess weight and that I do so without any difficulty. I will never feel hungry, because if hungry I must eat; I will never feel deprived of my favourite foods because they are waiting there for me to enjoy the next time I am hungry. I will never feel I cannot sit down with friends or family at a mealtime – but if I am not hungry, I will just enjoy a drink in their company, knowing I can eat whatever I like later on.

Because I understand the power of my subconscious mind and that whatever I imagine, I can achieve, I am going to use visualization to increase my chances of looking exactly as I would wish to look.

In my mind I see myself now, standing before a full-length mirror and looking exactly as I would like. I am wearing an outfit I would dearly love to wear but cannot get into at the moment. Perhaps it is something I used to wear, which no longer fits; perhaps it is the type of garment I always wished to wear but have never felt slim enough to do so; perhaps it is just a figment of my imagination. Whatever it is, I see my reflection in the mirror from the back, from the front, from the sides. At each angle, I look perfect in the garment of my choice. Nothing is stretching, nothing gaping – everything fits perfectly, just as it should. I am aware of absolute joy because I know that garment looks good on me and shows off my new figure to perfection. I know this is how I am going to look once I have lost my excess weight.

And now I remind myself of that feeling of having just eaten a good, enjoyable and satisfying meal. And I remember that this feeling is going to remain with me almost all the time until I repeat this script. Because of that, with every day that passes, I shall be getting slimmer, fitter, and happier.

Helpful affirmations

If you wish to incorporate affirmations into your weight-loss regime, the best ones to use are the following:
• I am becoming the shape and size I wish to be.

- I obey the three rules.
- I feel pleasantly full at almost all times.

SECOND STAGE

For many people the first script, if used regularly, will be all that is needed to lose excess weight. But some, especially those who have a great deal of weight to lose, might need the second stage.

It is well known that many people, especially if they are very overweight, will begin by losing weight well but will eventually reach a plateau when, even if they do everything correctly, their weight does not seem to budge. This happens because their body has grown used to the new regime and no longer seems to be responding to it. In fact, if these people were to continue using the same technique and accept the fact they will not see much in the way of a result for a few weeks, things would begin to move again and weight loss would recommence.

But human nature is not like that. If you know you are doing all that is expected of you and yet the scale reading doesn't seem to change, you are likely to become disheartened and give up, thinking perhaps that this 'plateau weight' is what you were meant to be. To prevent that happening and to ensure you don't give up until you have really become the size and shape you wish to be, this second-stage script is designed to give your weight loss a kick-start and get things moving again.

You don't have to abandon permanently what you have been doing until now – after all, it has been working, hasn't it? Just put it aside temporarily and use the following script until the scales show you have begun to lose weight again, then return to the original script and work with that. Remember, this script should always follow on from the initial induction and relaxation script you learned.

Because I have come to a point where my weight loss appears either to have slowed down or to have temporarily stopped altogether, I am going to change my script and my way of thinking for a short time.

I realize it is natural, especially when there is a considerable amount of weight to be lost, for such a plateau to be reached. And I know that, even if I simply continue to use the original script, I will soon start to lose weight again. But in order to restart that weight loss as soon as possible, I am going to use the following script.

I still begin by imagining I have just eaten a good and satisfying meal so that I feel pleasantly and comfortably full. And I still know that, whatever happens, I must continue to obey the same three, simple rules:
* *I will weigh myself once a week only.*
* *If I feel hungry, I know that I must eat.*
* *If I am not hungry, I know I must not eat anything at all.*

The difference comes when I do find myself feeling hungry and know that my body is telling me that food is necessary for my well-being.

As I relax now, I imagine I am standing before an enormous glass of pure, fresh drinking water. The glass is as tall as I am and it is full of water. There is a very large straw in this glass of water and now I imagine myself using that straw to drink all the water in the glass. It tastes clean and fresh and I enjoy the water as I drink it.

When I stop drinking and the glass is empty once more, I feel quite full again. Not completely full, because I know it is time for me to eat and take in nutrition, but the water ensures I am only slightly hungry rather than extremely so.

The next time I find myself feeling hungry, before I begin to eat whatever food I wish to consume I shall pour myself a normal-sized glass of water and I shall drink all the water in the glass before beginning to eat. The water will take the edge off my appetite and I will not wish to eat as much as usual.

I will be quite happy with this situation because I realize I can still eat whatever food I like best, and if I am not able to finish all I have prepared, I will not be deprived of anything I really enjoy – I simply have to wait until the next time I feel hungry.

And now, once again, I picture myself standing before that full-length mirror, looking at my own reflection. I am wearing something that really shows off my wonderful new shape and size. I look at myself from every angle, noticing that everything fits me perfectly and that nothing is stretched or gaping. The sight of my own body with its ideal shape and size excites me and fills me with happiness because I know this perfect shape and size is mine and will be so for as long as I wish.

A SLIP IS NOT A FAILURE

Because no one of us is a saint, there might come a time when we fall by the wayside a little. This is more likely to happen with weight loss than any other problem you might deal with by means of self-hypnosis because losing weight often takes a little longer than dealing with other problems. Some of the things I have heard people say on such occasions are: 'I have been on holiday and didn't use the technique for two weeks'; 'I went to dinner with friends and had to eat what was put in front of me'; 'I had some personal problems and, because I was feeling really miserable, I had a lot to eat, even though I knew I wasn't hungry'; or 'I don't know what came over me – I was in the shop and bought this enormous chocolate bar and ate the whole thing at once'. I'm sure you have heard – perhaps even said – something similar.

The thing to bear in mind is that even if you have lapsed in some small way, this doesn't make you a failure or mean that you won't be able to lose all that excess weight. It is just a small hiccup. That is, it is a small hiccup provided that once you realize what has happened you put it behind you, and go back to using your self-hypnosis technique and script.

What often happens when someone is on an ordinary diet – counting calories or points or carbohydrates, and so on – is they think to themselves, 'Well, I've ruined everything now. I'm never going to be able to lose weight. I might just as well go back to eating the way I did before.' If they do that, of course, they will be adding to their diet all those things they have been depriving themselves of for so long – and on goes that weight again.

For the person who has been using self-hypnosis to lose weight, however, it is quite different. You have not been depriving yourself of any of your favourite foods. There is nothing to reintroduce into your diet and therefore there is nothing to make you regain the weight you have already successfully lost. All that slight lapse will mean to you is that you might take a week or two longer to reach that ideal shape and size than you would have done if you had not deviated from the technique. Is that such a terrible thing? I think not. For one thing, if at the outset someone told you it would take, say, 46 weeks to lose all your excess weight, would it have made any real difference if they had told you it would take 48 weeks? Of course not. You would be so delighted that the excess weight was going to vanish forever that the precise number of weeks would not matter. Not only that but by the time you are within a week or two of reaching your ideal shape and size, will anyone realize you are perhaps a pound or two over the weight you are going to be? Can you tell when someone is two pounds overweight? Of course you can't.

Hopefully you will manage to reach your goal without any lapses along the way. But even if you do slip up, remember it is your attitude towards this slip that governs how much effect it will have on the final outcome. If you see it as a total failure, ruining everything you have been trying to achieve, you will become so disheartened that you are unlikely to progress with the technique you have been practising – and you probably will fail. If, however, you say to yourself, 'Okay, I slipped up but all that means is it might take me a week or two longer to reach my ideal, and that is not the end of the world. I will go back to the self-hypnosis technique straight away and will soon see the weight coming off again' then the lapse will have little or no relevance to you.

The joy of losing weight by means of self-hypnosis, as opposed to any other method, is that you are in control. You are not depriving yourself of anything you really like and you know that, once lost, that excess weight will never return.

6

Ongoing Problems

If you want to stop smoking or to reach a certain weight, once you have achieved that goal, the problem stops. But there are some problems that need to be controlled because it is often very difficult to eliminate them permanently: ongoing problems such as asthma and tinnitus, or recurring problems such as migraine and premenstrual syndrome (PMS). All these can be alleviated by self-hypnosis. In some people they can be completely cured, while in others the symptoms can be greatly reduced.

STRESS

Stress has been the buzzword for some years now and it is responsible for a great deal of unhappiness, for an enormous number of lost working days, and for considerable financial cost as litigation and demands for compensation increase.

Although the problem is commonly referred to as 'stress', what actually does the damage is *excess stress*. A certain amount of stress is essential in our lives, or we would not be able to get out of bed in the morning. It is stress that spurs us on, that enables us to think on our feet, to get out of tricky situations and pursue interesting lives. Excess stress, however, is debilitating in the extreme. It can lead to physical, mental or emotional breakdown. It can be responsible for difficulties in the workplace and in relationships.

In many cases, excess stress can be controlled in just 15 to 30 minutes of real relaxation a day. Ideally, of course, we should do all we can to eliminate the basic cause of that excess stress wherever possible. It may mean a change of job, trying to find extra help with problems, or escaping from a situation that distresses you. But there are instances where escape from a situation is just not possible. Even in such cases, however, self-hypnosis can help you to control the excess stress to such an extent that it no longer does you real harm.

Think of a pressure cooker, where the steam builds up as time goes on. If there was not a system of releasing some of that pent-up steam, there would probably be an explosion. But pressure cookers are designed with just such a release system. In the same way, when pressure is building up within you, you can help yourself by bringing it back down to a reasonable level each day. If you don't do this, you are building pressure upon pressure until your system will have its own type of explosion – and you will be the one to suffer.

Let's assume either that you are doing your best to reduce the amount of stress in your life or that you come to the conclusion there is little or nothing you can do about it. How are you going to bring about this desired reduction in your personal stress level? The answer lies in the following script, which you can use after the normal induction script you have already practised.

Script for stress reduction

Now that I am relaxed physically, I am going to imagine myself walking through a door into a very beautiful garden. It is a lovely summer's day – warm but not uncomfortably hot – and there is a warm and gentle breeze blowing.

This is a very large garden so I am not able to see all of it at once. The part I can see is bathed in sunlight. It is a bright and colourful area with short, green grass and beds full of brilliantly coloured and scented flowers. All my favourite flowers are there and, as I look, I am aware of bright butterflies dancing around them and soft, fluffy bumblebees darting from flower to flower as they collect the pollen.

I walk across the grass, feeling it short and crisp beneath my feet. As I pass between the flower beds, I am aware of the bright colours and the beautiful scent of the flowers growing there.

Now I come to a wooden arch with velvety roses twining around it. As I pass through the arch into the next part of the garden, I am very aware of the sweet scent of the roses and the softness of their petals.

Once through the arch, I find myself in another part of the garden. This area is softer, quieter and gentler. The grass is a little longer and softer beneath my feet. There are trees and bushes here so that long fingers of shadow trace patterns on the green grass. There are flowers here, too, but their colours are softer and more muted – gentle pinks, mauves and white.

This is a gentle garden, where birds sing among the fluttering leaves of the trees and a gentle breeze causes the scent of the flowers to fill the air.

In this quiet garden I come to an old wooden seat with some soft, faded cushions on it. I sit on the seat, feeling the cushions fit perfectly around my body in such a way that I know that this is my seat in my garden. Every time I sit on this seat, a feeling of peace and tranquillity comes over me.

From this part of the garden, as I sit on my seat I can see down into a green valley, where there are small groups of cottages and an old stone church.

Feeling at peace with myself and my world, I imagine all my problems being tied up in one big bundle and tossed away. They float off into the air above the valley, never to cause me trouble again. If and when I do think about them, it will be calmly and quietly and in such a way that I can deal with them as well as might be possible without letting them affect my own well-being.

I can sit here in my gentle garden for as long as I wish and I can return to it at any time. It is always here, waiting for me, and it will always bring me this sense of peace and tranquillity. When I open my eyes again and go about whatever I have to do, it will be in a calm and measured way without any undue tension or stress.

I am at peace… peace… peace.

Stress in relation to other problems

Various problems can be reduced in intensity by dealing with stress, even if they cannot be eliminated altogether. Eczema, tinnitus and psoriasis, for example, cannot be cured by self-hypnosis, but their symptoms can be drastically reduced after using the self-hypnosis script for stress relief. Stress may not be the deep-rooted cause of such problems, but it is certainly true that the problem itself causes the sufferer a great deal of stress. If this excess stress can be eliminated or even considerably reduced, the unpleasant symptoms will automatically diminish. So, if you suffer from one of these distressing problems, try using the self-hypnosis script for the reduction of stress and I think you will be pleasantly surprised by the way in which your symptoms are reduced.

INSOMNIA

Insomnia is a miserable condition. For some people it means being unable to get to sleep for hours after going to bed – lying there, tossing and turning and watching the hands of the clock creep towards morning. Others may drop off quite quickly, only to wake again two or three hours later and find it impossible to get back to sleep. Whatever form of insomnia someone suffers from, the effects carry over through the day as that person becomes more and more tired, and less and less able to cope with their daily tasks.

Insomnia is also one of the most self-perpetuating of conditions. Anyone who has a single bad night's sleep will usually make up for it the following night. The chronic insomniac, however, will go to bed convinced that they will not be able to get to sleep. This in turn will make them tense and anxious and therefore far less likely to go to sleep. Yet insomnia is one of the easiest conditions to cure by means of self-hypnosis. Provided there is no underlying health condition that causes difficulty in sleeping, it should not take more than a few weeks to put an end to the problem for good. Before you think about using a script, though, there are a few changes in lifestyle that you might find helpful. These include such things as:

• Try to establish a pre-bedtime routine. You might like to have a warm bath, go for a walk, put out the milk bottles, read a magazine, and so on. But if you get into the habit of doing the same thing every night, it is like sending a message to your subconscious mind saying, 'I'm getting ready to go to bed now.'

- Avoid doing anything too stimulating just before going to bed – whether it is watching a thriller on television, reading an exciting novel, drinking coffee or alcohol. (Alcohol might help you to get to sleep initially but you will soon wake up again.)
- If you are someone who tends to lie there thinking of all the things you have to do next day and worrying in case you forget them, keep a notepad and pen by your bed. Then, if something is really on your mind, you can jot down a reminder and relax.

Insomnia script

As I lie here in bed, I am fully relaxed and happy in the knowledge that I shall be able to drift peacefully into sleep and that my sleep will be deep and untroubled until I wake in the morning.

In my imagination I am lying back in a small, safe boat, which is drifting along a gentle river. As I look around me I can see bright blue sky, brilliant green grass and leaves touched by the gold of the midday sun. It is midday and the sun is high overhead but it is not unpleasantly hot and here, on my river, a gentle breeze is blowing. I feel very happy to be here as I float down the river in my boat, listening to birds singing overhead.

Now my little boat drifts onward, further along that same gently flowing river. It is later in the day and the colours around me are softer and more muted. Long fingers of shadow are cast on the water by the trees above. Although it is still warm, there is none of the strong heat of the day. The birds are beginning to sing their evening song and I listen to it as I drift ever onward.

It is night-time on my river. My little boat is surrounded by shadows. The sky is dark except for the glow of the moon and the twinkling of the stars. The birds and bees have fallen silent and all I can hear is the gentle lapping of the water on the sides of the boat. I am filled with a sense of peace and tranquillity. I am safe and contented, and can stay here as long as I wish. I breathe deeply, breathing in the perfect peace

that surrounds me.
   All is quiet… all is still… all is peace.

Case study: Norma

Norma never experienced any difficulty with sleeping until she was in her late twenties. At that time she was promoted within the company she worked for – something she had hoped would happen and had looked forward to with keen anticipation. Her parents repeatedly told her how proud they were of her achievement. Far from being the exciting challenge she had hoped for, Norma found her new position brought with it extreme stress and pressure. She felt isolated from her former colleagues and her senior manager seemed to expect far more of her than it was possible for her to achieve. She was naturally disappointed but also felt unable to confide in anyone as she thought she would be letting them all down.

She began to find it difficult to sleep. She would lie there, worrying about the day that was over and fretting even more about the one that was yet to come. The lack of sleep made her tired and she began to make silly mistakes at work. No one else seemed to notice and she was able to put them right, but this took up much of her precious time, leaving her even less in which to carry out her work.

Eventually Norma came to her senses. She realized she could not carry on in this way and changed her job, going to one where she was far happier and far more able to cope. But even though the pressure had now been removed, insomnia had become a habit. The more she went to bed thinking, 'I really must get some sleep tonight', the more elusive that sleep became. She reached the stage where she would lie in bed crying in frustration because of her inability to sleep.

It was then that a friend introduced her to self-hypnosis. The philosophy behind it seemed to make sense and, because she was extremely unwilling to take medication to help her sleep in case it was addictive, she decided to give the technique a try. By using a self-made cassette every night, Norma was soon able to relax and, finally, to get to sleep. Just three weeks after starting to use her tape, Norma's insomnia was a thing of the past. But she knew that should it ever return, however briefly, she now had the means of eliminating it.

ASTHMA

Asthma can have many causes. Sometimes it starts as the result of an allergy, sometimes because of a physical problem an individual may have been born with, sometimes as a result of an emotional trauma in the life of the sufferer. The degree of suffering endured can also vary from person to person. One asthmatic may have nothing more than an irritating cough, which never seems to go away, while another may be troubled with long-lasting, and often very frightening, full-blown attacks necessitating the use of inhalers, regular medication and even hospitalization. And there are many stages in between.

If the asthma is caused by an allergy or by some physical malfunction in the sufferer, hypnotherapy (whether self-hypnosis or from a professional therapist) will not completely cure it. What it can do is dramatically reduce the incidence and severity of the attacks. In the case of asthma caused by an emotional trauma, not only are the attacks reduced but it is also possible to help the sufferer to rid themselves of it completely. If you suffer from the emotionally-based type of asthma, using the script suggested in a later chapter dealing with overcoming trauma will help you a great deal. But whichever the type of asthmatic you may be, the first thing to deal with is the number and severity of the attacks you experience.

To suffer an asthma attack is not only uncomfortable and distressing, it can be absolutely terrifying. If your attack is a bad one, you may feel you will never be able to catch your breath and breathe easily again. This, quite naturally, induces a sense of panic – which in turn can cause you to hyperventilate, and so the attack gets worse and worse. Regular use of the stress-relief script can help make your attacks less frequent. If you incorporate into that script the 'fixing' or 'anchoring' technique described in an earlier chapter, you will have something that will help you if you begin to experience the onset of an attack.

What usually happens is that if a sufferer gets the feeling they are about to have an attack, the reaction, understandably, is one of panic. No one wants to go through a frightening and exhausting experience. If at the first sign of an attack you use the 'fixing' technique of putting your finger and thumb tips together, and pressing and releasing them three times, it is likely to calm your breathing sufficiently for you to deal with the situation. You may decide to use a prescribed inhaler or you may be able to sit quietly for some moments and, with the increased sense of relaxation you feel, be able to regulate your breathing so that the dreaded attack never actually arrives.

However, if you are someone who suffers from asthma it is important that you practise both the stress-relief script and the fixing technique regularly rather than wait for the moment of an attack – when you may find it much harder to think clearly – to put it into action.

Breathing exercise
Most asthma sufferers – indeed most people – do not breathe properly most of the time. Breathing should come from the diaphragm but the majority of people spend much of the time taking shallow breaths from the upper chest. Not only does this mean we are getting insufficient oxygen to the brain, but also given any panic situation we are likely to hyperventilate and this, taken to extremes, can even cause us to pass out.

Just as any physical function of the body can be improved by means of regular exercise, so can our ability to breathe properly. This is important for everyone but even more so for those who suffer from the breathing problems incorporated in asthma. This exercise need not take more than ten minutes a day but can make a great deal of difference to the frequency and strength of an asthma attack:

1. Lie on your back on the floor, with your head resting on five, average-sized paperback books. Place the soles of your feet flat on the floor and bend your knees so that they point towards the ceiling. Close your eyes.

2. Place your hands gently over your ribcage so that your fingertips touch lightly together.

3. Breathe in slowly, allowing your fingertips to be forced apart by the movement of your body. As you breathe out again, your fingers should return to the original position. (Let all this happen naturally – don't try and force your fingers to move.)

4. Continue in this way for five or ten minutes (you can have some relaxing music playing at the same time if you wish).

5. Stop and sit up very slowly. This is important because, particularly if this exercise is new to you, you may find you feel a little dizzy when you sit up. If so, remain sitting for a few moments until the dizziness passes and you can get to your feet. After a few days of practising this exercise, the dizziness will not occur unless you have been very stressed. But to be on the safe side, it is best always to sit and then stand quite slowly.

MIGRAINE

There are two basic types of migraine. The first arises because of some sort of allergy – the most common culprits being coffee, red wine and chocolate. So, if you are a migraine sufferer it is as well to be aware of whether these – or some other substance – might play a part in your suffering. If so, the answer is fairly obvious and the offending substance must be cut out of your life.

The other most common form of migraine is caused by a reaction to excess stress. If this applies to you then, as a first stage, I would certainly recommend using the script given at the start of this chapter for dealing with excess stress. You know how frequently you are likely to suffer from migraine. If regular use of the script for excess stress reduces the number of attacks, you will know you are well on the way to dealing with the problem.

Most migraine sufferers are only too aware of the early signs of the onset of an attack. As with asthmatics, the fear of an intense attack naturally causes sufferers to become more tense, more stressed – and therefore far more likely to suffer an even more severe attack. If you are able to recognize those early warning signs, there is a script that can prove really useful in making that attack disappear before it even arrives. In the worst cases, this can help to avoid all those miserable days spent lying in a darkened room, waiting for the symptoms of nausea, eye pain or headache to go away. As with all the other scripts, this script should follow on from the original induction and relaxation script.

Migraine script

As I lie here calm and relaxed, I imagine a piece of pink ice placed on my forehead.

Because of the warmth of my forehead compared with the piece of ice, the ice slowly begins to melt. As it does so, cooling trickles of pale pink water run to the sides of my forehead, cooling my temples.

The ice continues to melt and the water gently runs around the sockets of my eyes, cooling them, and then to the pulse area behind my ears. My head feels so cool and I feel myself relax even more.

From the pulse areas behind my ears, this cool pink water gently and slowly continues on its way to the sides of my neck and then, slowly and soothingly, to the back of my neck.

The ice has completely melted now and as I feel the cooling dampness dry on my skin, the temperature of my skin reduces to a pleasant level, my pulse rate reduces, and my head and eyes feel wonderfully clear. The healing pink ice has done its work and my mind is at peace. I feel fit, strong and clear-headed.

Because I know I can use this technique whenever I wish – and because I know it will always cause those early signs to disappear – I know I am now in control of my life again and I need never suffer another migraine attack. I am free.

The only type of migraine it is difficult to cure by this method is one that is already there, full-strength, when the sufferer wakes up in the morning. Because they were asleep during those early warning signs, they were not aware of them and were therefore not able to put the technique into practice before the attack became a full-blown one. If this applies to you, and if you are aware of the approximate frequency of such attacks, you need to use the script before going to sleep the night before. If you have no idea of when the next attack is likely to be, it certainly cannot do any harm to practise the script every night to ensure you are fully prepared to dispel the attack, whenever it might arrive.

An interesting fact I have noted over the years of working with those who suffer from migraine is that, once they feel they are in control of the situation, they become so empowered that in many cases the migraine attacks disappear altogether, and even those early warning signs become a thing of the past. For the others, who know they need never suffer more than those early warning signs, using this self-hypnosis script can bring a sense of peace and serenity they thought they had lost for ever.

PMT AND THE MENOPAUSE

There are various problems that can arise as women experience either their monthly cycle or the menopause. If you have any physical problems that give cause for concern, you should of course consult your medical practitioner for advice. But many of the problems can be dealt with extremely effectively by self-hypnosis.

First, the emotional problems brought about by the tremendous fluctuation in the hormonal state, which can definitely be treated and overcome by hypnosis. Such problems are often self-perpetuating in that they cause you to feel extremely stressed, and when anyone is under stress the body automatically produces more adrenaline to help cope with whatever situation may have caused that stress. When a woman's body produces that adrenaline boost, the production of female hormones is automatically reduced. This, of course, only serves to increase and intensify any menstrual upsets she may already be experiencing.

If you know that you always become short-tempered, depressed, agitated, or suffer emotionally in any other way prior to your monthly cycle, you can reduce these feelings by using the excess-stress script given earlier in this chapter. It is as well to start using the script three or four days before your period would normally begin so that your mind and body have had time to react to it before it starts.

Then there is the physical pain, which can be anything from stomach cramps to headaches – with many other symptoms in between. At the end of this chapter you will find a script for pain relief, but bear in mind that this should only ever be used once you have confirmed with your doctor that the pain does not need medical attention. If, as in many cases, you are told it is 'just one of those things' that accompanies menstruation and all you are offered are standard painkillers then you will probably find the pain-relief script quite sufficient.

The script for dealing with excess stress is also ideal for those women who are going through the menopause, particularly those who suffer from hot flushes and headaches. Because you will be reducing the amount of adrenaline your body is producing, your hormones are more likely to adjust themselves to an appropriate level for your well-being and this should reduce – if not eliminate – all those dreaded symptoms. If this applies to you, it is advisable to use the script daily until you feel sure the menopause, with its attendant discomforts, is well behind you.

It has been found that in some cases, though it does not always apply, continued use of self-hypnosis after the cessation of the menopause can enable women to manage without the use of HRT or any other prescribed substance.

PAIN RELIEF

Pain is usually there for a reason. It is an indication that something is not as it should be. If you have regular, constant or unexplained pain, the first thing you must do is to consult your doctor to see if an explanation can be found, and if medical treatment is needed. Even a simple headache may be an indication of something more. Of course, it may be just what it seems – a simple headache – but it could also mean you need to have your eyes tested or, given a worse scenario, that you have a brain tumour. So it is essential you discover the reason for your pain before turning to self-hypnosis for help.

Another reason for pain could be to prevent you doing something that could cause you more harm. If you have a broken ankle, for example, the pain you feel when putting your foot to the ground will prevent you putting too much weight on it, thereby causing further damage. So it would be foolish – and probably dangerous – to remove that pain by means of self-hypnosis.

However, some pains are the result of the excess stress we were talking about before. There is a saying that 'Every thought has a physical response' and this is true. If I ask you to think about a lovely holiday you have had, your body will relax, you are likely to smile and even to experience a greater sense of well-being than before. If, however, I mention something you really dislike – such as spiders or snakes for some people – your muscles will automatically become more tense and you will feel a sense of unease, even when it is only the word that has been mentioned and the offending creature is not present.

People who are regularly under stress, for whatever reason, experience muscular tension on a daily basis. It may present itself in the form of backache, headaches, grinding of teeth, or in many other ways. It may lead to ulcers, constipation or diarrhoea. If your medical practitioner can assure you that any such symptoms you suffer is the result of excess stress, as opposed to an underlying medical condition, then the pain-relief script may be for you. The script is also useful for those who have chronic pain for which the explanation is known but which cannot be alleviated.

Pain-relief script
This script is only suitable if your doctor has told you that you do not need any medical treatment and that relieving the pain will not do you any further harm, or if you know the cause of the pain and it is soon to be removed. If you do decide it is appropriate for you, remember that, as ever, it is designed to be used after the initial induction script.

I am feeling very calm and relaxed, and I am happy because I know

*that, using the power of my own mind, I can bring about relief from the
pain that has been troubling me.*

*I focus my attention now on the central point of that pain and, as I do
so, I imagine the pain is in fact a hard, red round cricket ball. I see that
ball in my mind... the ball of pain. It is red, it is hard, it is warm, and it
is at the very centre of my pain.*

*Slowly, very slowly, I imagine that ball moving away from the centre
of the pain in the direction of the nearest arm or leg. Inch by inch, it
moves. Slowly, the ball moves through my body and, as it does so, it takes
with it the pain that has been surrounding it.*

*Very, very slowly I imagine this hard, red ball moving on until it
reaches the top of the nearest arm or leg.*

Now continue by selecting one of the two following options:

1. *The ball is at the top of my arm, inside my arm. I imagine it moving, so slowly, down my arm until it is just above my elbow. When I can
imagine it there, I move it slowly further down my arm, taking as long
as it takes, until it is just above my wrist. Now, still very slowly, the
hard red ball enters my hand. In order to travel down my fingers, that
ball must break up into five pieces, or even disintegrate into a myriad of
dust particles. When it has done so, these pieces or particles travel down
my fingers and thumb and I visualize them coming out of my fingers and
disappearing into the atmosphere. By using the power of my own mind,
I have enabled my body to rid itself of the pain it used to feel and I have
obtained the relief I so desired.*

2. *I imagine this hard red ball moving, very, very slowly down my
thigh until it is just above my knee. Once I can imagine it in that
position, I move it slowly further down my leg, taking as long as is
needed, until that hard red ball is just above my ankle. Now I imagine it
moving, very, very slowly, into my foot. Then, in order to pass through
my toes and out of my body, that hard red ball must break up into five
pieces or even disintegrate in hundreds of particles of dust. Having done
so, these pieces or particles enter into my toes and I visualize them
leaving the tips of my toes and disappearing into the atmosphere, leaving
my body completely. By using the power of my own mind, I have enabled*

my body to rid itself of the pain it used to feel and I have obtained the relief I so desired.

Case study: James

James was a highly successful, wealthy businessman who came to see me about ten years ago. He was owner and managing director of a large organization and had many people working for him. He was married with three teenage children, and would have enjoyed both his work and his private life but for one thing.

About two years before I met him James had been out riding when he fell badly from his horse, injuring his back. A period of traction, surgery and physiotherapy followed and the spine was repaired as well as possible with the insertion of a metal plate. Ever since that time James had suffered from constant back pain, for which his doctor and consultant assured him nothing could be done apart from the prescription of strong medical painkillers. But James felt these dulled his thinking and, in any case, he really did not want to be taking prescribed drugs for the rest of his life.

When I met him, James told me he could cope with the pain during the day because he was so busy and involved in his company that he was almost able to put it from his mind. What he could not cope with, however, were the nights. He would lie awake for hours, unable to find a position comfortable enough for sleep and with nothing to think of except how much his back was hurting him. This lack of sleep, not unnaturally, caused him to be tired during the day and he felt this prevented him from giving of his best at work.

What James wanted, therefore, was a technique that would enable him to relieve the pain sufficiently for him to get a good night's sleep and wake refreshed in the morning. I checked with James' doctor that to give him such relief would not cause him any further damage and was assured that this was so. Using the pain-relief script, James was able to achieve the sleep and rest he so needed.

Another person for whom this script was suitable was a woman who was awaiting a hysterectomy operation. She knew the cause of her pain and she knew her operation was just a few weeks away. What she needed was something to help her cope with the days until that operation, and for her too the pain-relief script fulfilled that need.

7

Fears and Phobias

Initially it may seem difficult to explain the difference between a fear and a phobia – indeed it is not uncommon for the root cause of either to be the same. But the dictionary describes a phobia as 'an irrational fear'. So while it may be sensible and common to take precautions in potentially dangerous or difficult situations, the extreme panic aroused in the phobia sufferer is not common and causes both sufferer and those who care about them great distress. And when it comes to some of the more unusual phobias – a fear of the number thirteen, perhaps, or a fear of being cold, a fear of Mondays or a fear of feathers – these are more difficult for the onlooker to understand.

It is also possible that what starts out as a 'normal' fear can eventually become a phobia. Each time we repeat to ourselves that we are frightened of something, we reinforce that fear. Say it often enough and we convince our subconscious mind so effectively that should that something come into our life, we feel a sense of panic and foreboding.

Not only does a phobic suffer the anguish of the phobia attack itself, they also have to cope with a sense of feeling 'stupid', 'inadequate', 'different' or 'cowardly'. Those are all words I have heard phobia sufferers using about themselves when telling me about their condition. In many instances they have been told to 'snap out of it' and feel ashamed that they are unable to do so. Or perhaps some well-meaning person has insisted on confronting them with whatever it is they fear in the hope that a taste of reality will disperse the anxiety forever. This never works and the well-meaning individual is in fact increasing the hold that the phobia has over the sufferer.

It has even been known for some therapists to use 'aversion therapy' to try and cure a phobia. This also involves confronting the sufferer with whatever they dread – and it is doomed to failure, particularly if the phobic person is suddenly faced with the object without any prior warning.

Of course, there are some phobias that need never impact on your life. If you happen to be terrified and panic-stricken at the thought of being on top of a mountain, for example, you can live the rest of your life quite happily without ever having to face that situation. But should your fear be of something far more common, it can ruin your life. No phobia ever stands still. If nothing is done to deal with the situation, you can be sure the phobia will get worse in time. This is partly because of the effect of repetition on the subconscious mind, as mentioned before. But also, once the subconscious is satisfied that you are a phobic, it will persuade your imagination to come up with stronger and stronger images to terrify you.

In these days of frequent intercontinental travel, it is easy to see how a phobia of flying can be inconvenient and can spoil holidays not only for the sufferer but for their immediate family, who might ultimately decide it best not to travel by air. It may be more difficult to understand how a fear of feathers is going to trouble your life greatly. After all, you don't have to buy a hat with feathers on, keep a budgerigar, or use a quill pen. But all birds have feathers and, while you might not choose to approach a bird too closely, it is very hard to avoid them completely when walking down the street. Suddenly an everyday occurrence, such as walking into town or round the park, becomes a situation to be dreaded, and it becomes essential to keep a wary eye out for any birds that may be near or may be encountered. If no help is forthcoming and the situation is taken to extremes, over time the person with a phobia about feathers may become a prisoner their own home, afraid to go out in case they encounter a bird in their vicinity. The bird does not have to approach them or take off and fly – the very fact that it is nearby is enough to cause a panic situation.

HOW PHOBIAS ARISE

Phobias can develop for many different reasons. They can be inherited, for example, as in the case of Phoebe. Her mother had always been terrified of thunderstorms, though no one knew the reason for this fear as nothing dreadful had ever happened to her during a storm. When Phoebe was a tiny baby in her pram, if a thunderstorm threatened her mother would run frantically from room to room, closing curtains against the sight of any lightening and turning mirrors to the wall (something her own mother had always done, believing something terrible would happen if lightening was reflected in a mirror). She would play the radio loudly to drown out the sound of any thunderclaps and pick up her baby, clutching her as if to protect her from the terrible weather invasion.

It is not difficult to understand how all this panic affected the young Phoebe. Not only was she automatically aware of all the 'precautions' being taken against the thunderstorm when her mother picked her up, she could actually feel the rapid heartbeat, the sweaty hands, the shallow breathing of her mother. Not only is a baby extremely sensitive to the emotions that surround it at any given time, but to a small child mother is always right. So if mother reacted in such a way to the onset of a thunderstorm, such a reaction must be the correct one. Without being able to put all this into rational thought, the baby automatically learns to mimic mother's reactions. As she grew older, Phoebe never stopped to wonder why she reacted as she did. Having inherited the extreme fear at a very early age, it was something she had always done and something she therefore continued to do until such time when she decided to do something about the situation.

A phobia can arise because of a situation in the sufferer's past. Take as an example a group of children playing in the school playground during break time. A little boy chases a group of small girls with a wriggling worm held in his hand. It doesn't matter that a worm cannot actually do you any harm – the girls scream and run away, each one's scream encouraging the others to react in the same way. The boy manages to run up to one of the girls and perhaps drops the worm onto her hand, in her hair or down the neck of her dress. While this is probably doing far more harm to the poor worm than to the girl, nonetheless to the child this is a horror scenario and quite sufficient to set up a fear of having a worm in close proximity – or even of seeing one nearby – which can easily develop into a phobia if nothing is done about it.

Apologies if you think this is a dreadfully sexist example, but it does still happen in that way. In fact, if it were to happen the other way around and the girl goaded the boy, the outcome might not be the same. A boy will not want to appear cowardly before his friends and, even if he doesn't like the situation, he will probably pretend he doesn't care. Therefore he will not be sowing the seeds of panic. Small girls still have a tendency to react in groups. You have only to think of the way they will all scream for the same pop star, share crushes on the same teacher, or terrify each other by vowing they are certain they have just failed a vital exam. So the hysteria at the dreaded worm will pass quickly from one to the other, each scream of panic reinforcing the fact that the worm is something to be feared so that its unfortunate recipient believes something terrible has happened to her when the worm does eventually touch her.

Other phobias have a basis in reality. It is very common for someone to have a fear of flying. While self-hypnosis can deal with this situation and help the sufferer to be happier about travelling in an aeroplane, it is not possible to state categorically that the plane will not crash. You can point out that compared with the number of worldwide flights made each day, the number of those that crash is minute. You can produce figures to show that it is far more dangerous to travel in a car – or even to cross the road on foot – but you cannot promise that the plane they happen to be going on will definitely arrive safely at its destination.

DEALING WITH PHOBIAS

In this chapter you will discover how to deal with any type of phobia, as each one requires a slightly different approach. You will learn how to create progressive scripts so that you can deal with the situation as it gradually improves.

There are basically three types of phobia sufferers. One does not care how and why they developed the phobia – they just want to be free of it. This is the person who can say, 'I know I have a phobia. I have no idea how or why it arose in me but I am an adult and I don't want it to be part of my life any more.' Another phobic will be aware of the initial cause of the problem, even though it may have been many, many years earlier. The third type of sufferer will not know the original cause of their phobia but will have a desperate need to know, believing they will not be able to rid themselves of the phobia satisfactorily unless they have all the knowledge at their fingertips.

The first two types of phobia sufferers can be easily cured by self-hypnosis, while the third requires the help of a professional hypnotherapist. Using simple techniques, it is possible to take the sufferer back in time to the action or event that is the underlying cause of the current phobia. This is not a painful process and will probably only take a single session but it is not something you can do for yourself. On its own, this knowledge will not be sufficient to cure the phobia. It is still necessary to go on and do that by means of hypnotherapy or self-hypnosis. But for those to whom it matters, finding out why you developed a phobia in the first place may sometimes be helpful. As one man told me, 'Knowing why I developed my fear in the first place helped to convince me that I was just like other people and not going mad. There was a reason for my fear, so I am not stupid for having it.'

Remember that whichever type of phobia sufferer you are, the aim of dealing with it is not to make you actively love whatever it is you have previously been afraid of. It is to make you able to tolerate it and to deal with it as and when necessary, without any feelings of dread or panic.

INHERITED PHOBIAS

For the purposes of this script, I am going to use the situation described in this chapter – that of a person who has inherited a fear of thunderstorms from their mother. You can easily adapt this script to fit in with your particular circumstances.

As I relax both mentally and physically, I find great relief in the knowledge that the fear I have of thunderstorms is not just an illogical condition. I realise that, when I was a very small child, I picked up this feeling from my mother because of her own anxieties.

I do not blame my mother for this. She, too, was a victim of her own upbringing and something must have caused her to experience excessive fear whenever a thunderstorm occurred. I do not know what this was, and probably she never knew it either, but I understand how it can happen and realize she was not to blame, either for experiencing the fears or for passing them on to me.

Now that I understand the reason for my fear, there is nothing to prevent me from dealing with and overcoming it. And once it has been dealt with, it need never occur in my life again. That thought makes me very happy.

Obviously there are sensible precautions to be taken during a thunderstorm – not to take shelter beneath a tree when lightening is around, for example. But provided I bear these precautions in mind, I realize there is really very little a thunderstorm can do to harm me.

To prove this to myself, I choose to allow myself to imagine such a storm now. I visualize the flashes of lightening outside the window and at some distance. As I do so, I am aware that my body is very, very relaxed. My breathing is slow and even, and I know this lightening is not going to harm me in any way. It will light up the world outside for brief intervals and I am free to decide whether or not to look at and see its beauty. Whichever choice I make is fine and, because I have made this choice, I will still be very calm and very relaxed

Thunderstorms are usually accompanied by heavy rain, so now I imagine the rain pouring down outside in the garden. I am perfectly relaxed still, especially as I am aware how essential natural water is to the land outside.

During the thunderstorm I am imagining, there are loud claps of thunder. With each one I relax more and more. It is nothing more than noise. If I find it difficult to have loud noises around me, I can play some music and concentrate on this so that the noise is less obtrusive. Or I may choose to listen to the thunderclaps, knowing they are simply a sign of nature and can do me no harm. My breathing remains even and regular. I can choose how I react to a thunderstorm and therefore I am in control of the situation once more.

A thunderstorm need never bother me again because I can choose how I react to it rather than follow the inherited pattern that has previously caused difficulty for me.

Helpful affirmations
- I understand the cause of my phobia and unconditionally forgive the person who caused it in me.
- I am in control and can choose how I react to a thunderstorm.
- I choose to remain in control of my life.

PHOBIAS WHERE THE UNDERLYING CAUSE IS KNOWN

Here I shall use the example of the worm phobia caused by the actions of another child at school.

As I relax and allow myself to think clearly, I realize that my excessive fear of worms has an underlying cause whose origins are far in the past.

The original incident was a piece of mischief, not of malice. Small boy will often tease little girls with something they find unpleasant – and little girls will usually react by showing nervousness or horror. This was a very common situation but I have allowed it to build up in my mind until it has become of great importance.

I imagine myself now walking in the garden. I am walking across short, green grass, surrounded by flower beds. The ground is a little damp, as it has been raining. I walk to the edge of the lawn to examine the flowers growing in the beds. They are of many different colours and shapes, and all my favourite flowers are there.

As I study these flowers, I also see the rich darkness of the earth and perhaps a few small stones. Making its way across the earth, between the flowers, is a small worm. It is at some distance from me and is sliding away from me, so I feel quite at ease, relaxed and comfortable. I look at the flowers once more.

I am going to repeat this visualization every day until I feel perfectly happy with the image and know that I can go into the garden and watch a worm from a reasonable distance away, still feeling calm and relaxed.

When you feel comfortable with the concept, try going into a garden or a park and looking at the flowers growing in the beds there. See if you can spot a worm (not always easy) and observe its progress, realizing that, all the time, you remain perfectly calm. Once you can do that, adapt your script to include, say, bending down to look at the flowers and the worm more closely. Continue until you can do this in reality. Perhaps a final adaptation might include coming across a worm unexpectedly as it makes its way across a path. Practise this visualization in the same way until you feel able to do it in reality. In time you will find you are able to deal with seeing a worm with no worries whatsoever. You may not love the creature, and you probably won't want to handle it – but there is no need to do so. Nothing compares to the joy of having used the power of your own mind to help you overcome something that used to be a crippling fear or phobia.

PHOBIAS WHOSE CAUSE YOU FEEL THE NEED TO DISCOVER

As mentioned earlier, to go back in your life to discover the cause of a fear or phobia is something that should not be tackled alone but with the assistance of a professional hypnotherapist. However, once you are aware of that cause, you have the choice of either staying with that therapist until the problem no longer exists or, if you prefer, creating your own script for overcoming the phobia yourself.

PHOBIAS WITH AN APPARENTLY LOGICAL BASIS

Into this category fall such fears as a phobia about fire, about flying, about climbing ladders – or anything that may be potentially dangerous.

Fear of flying

Fear of flying is not always what it seems. Take Helena, for example. For as long as she could remember, Helena had known she was terrified of flying. She had only taken one holiday that necessitated air travel and this was when, newly married, she had gone with her husband to Spain for a summer break. She had been nervous on the outward journey but as it was her first, she had not realized in advance how dreadful she would find it. She was only able to make the return flight by drinking so much alcohol that she was unaware of a great deal of what was happening, and in fact slept for most of the journey. However, not being a great drinker, she paid for this on her return by feeling ill for the next couple of days. All future holidays taken by the couple, and later with their children, involved trains, ships, cars, coaches – anything but planes. Now, many years later, Helena's daughter had married an American and was based in New England. Helena was desperate to be able to fly out to see her daughter regularly.

The first thing to be done when confronted by someone who professes to have a fear of flying is to find out just what it is they are frightened of. For one person (although this, perhaps surprisingly, is the least common reason given) it could be a fear of the plane crashing or even being hijacked. Others really hate the sense of having no control over what is going to happen. Quite often the cause, as it turned out to be in Helena's case, is claustrophobia – the fear of being shut up in a plane for several hours with no means of escape.

If you suffer from a fear of flying, do take the time, first of all, to find out precisely what aspect it is that scares you. The scripts you prepare will be different in each case.

Set a date

However long you may have had a fear of flying and however much you may wish to overcome it, there is little to be gained by treating yourself using self-hypnosis unless you know a date you might be flying. How else will you be able to prove to yourself that it has worked? If you don't know when you are going to fly then, even if you are doing everything correctly, there may be a day when you are feeling a bit low and on such a day it wouldn't take much to convince yourself you did it all wrong, and it isn't going to work. So wait until you have planned a trip, then set to work. Ideally you should give yourself at least a month to deal with the problem. It is sometimes possible to overcome the fear a little more quickly but that could prove more difficult.

Once you have a date in mind, you need to think carefully about when you usually start to feel anxious. For some people it starts the moment the tickets have been booked, whereas others may feel quite calm until they are actually boarding the plane itself. The fears can begin at any time and, if you are to succeed in controlling them, you need to know at which point to start. Once you are aware of your first anxious moment, you can begin the desensitization process, taking it one stage at a time. Desensitization simply implies visualizing the feared thing (in this case, the flight) and imagining yourself drawing nearer and nearer to it, while maintaining that sense of deep relaxation you learned about in the beginning.

Let's suppose you are one of the more severe cases and your anxieties start to show themselves once the plane tickets have been booked. What would be your proposed plan of campaign?

1. Create a script for yourself that enables you to look forward with keen anticipation to the reason for your trip, whether it is a lovely holiday or a visit to people you really want to see. Always following on from the original relaxation technique, use this script regularly so that you convince your subconscious mind this is something you are really looking forward to.

2. Once you feel comfortable with that image, go on to script a visualization of the airport itself. See for yourself the check-in posts, the shops, bars and restaurants, and the people milling around, pushing their luggage trollies. Practise this script regularly until you feel quite relaxed and at ease when visualizing it. If time and distance make it possible, you might choose to visit the airport in order to reassure yourself that simply being there poses no further threat to you.

3. Now imagine yourself climbing the steps of the plane. Of course, you won't be able to put this into practice in advance in order to see that you can cope. But you will cope because the more you see it in your mind, the more your subconscious will be convinced you have really done all this before in a cool and relaxed way.

4. The last visualization is to imagine the flight as it will be – putting on your safety belt, the plane taking off, the gentle hum of its engine, the views of the clouds outside. Play it through like a video in your mind right up to the moment of the plane landing and you and the other passengers walking through its open door and back onto the safe, solid ground.

Other aids
It might help if you incorporate into your script the anchoring or fixing technique you learned at the outset as this will give you a sense of instant calm if you feel you need it when you actually make the flight. Another aid many people have found beneficial is to take a recording of the script with them, possibly with some gentle background music, so they are able to help themselves relax once the flight is under way.

An important reminder
Many people work really hard and successfully to be able to cope well with airline flights but forget to prepare for the return journey. Take the case of Alan, for example. He had been making journeys by air for several years as part of his career. He had never told anyone of his great fear of being on a plane and had usually coped by drinking himself into oblivion from the moment he was on board. Not only did this tend to dehydrate him so he felt terrible on arrival but it did not do a great deal for his negotiating capacities when he arrived.

Having decided he could not go on this way, Alan learned about self-hypnosis and, using his self-prepared script, he successfully dealt with the problem. In fact he contacted me afterwards to say he had positively enjoyed a flight to central Europe. He was there for about ten days conducting business and in all that time he never gave a thought to the journey home. Then, as he approached the check-in desk in readiness for the return flight, the old anxieties reared their heads again. It is true they were not nearly as severe as they had been in the past, but they were present nonetheless.

If you are travelling abroad by air for the first time since using self-hypnosis to conquer your fears, it is as well to spend ten minutes a day preparing in the same way for the return journey. You won't have to go on doing this forever. Once you have made two or three successful flights, your mind will become so convinced that this is how flights are, you will not need to spend so much time preparing in advance. It can never do any harm, however, to carry your relaxation tape with you and use it if it helps to build your confidence in your ability to cope with the flight successfully.

An in-flight script

Now that I am in my seat, I am aware of how deeply relaxed I feel. Every muscle, bone and sinew in my body has relaxed greatly. My mind is at peace as I concentrate on this script and on how I intend to behave.

As the engine of the plane starts up, its humming sound takes me deeper and deeper into relaxation. I can choose whether to close my eyes or to let them remain open for a while. I am aware of people around me, of the other travellers and the stewards and stewardesses working for the airline.

Now, as the journey gets under way, I close my eyes completely and let the monotonous sounds of the throbbing engine make me ever more relaxed. I am so deeply relaxed that I feel almost as though I am floating – a truly pleasant sensation.

Because I have practised it in advance, I know I can use the fixing technique whenever I wish. If I begin to feel the slightest bit nervous, I simply put together the first finger and the thumb of each hand, then press them together gently but firmly three times, and any nervousness floats away for ever.

As the journey progresses, I feel more and more at ease without needing any artificial relaxant, such as medication or alcohol. I experience the delightful sense of empowerment as I realize I am now in control and there is nothing that can cause me fear or upset.

I know that, once we have landed, and especially if this is my first flight since using self-hypnosis, I should remember to practise my deep relaxation technique daily for at least ten minutes. This will ensure I am also in a state of relaxation when I travel back.

Using the power of my own mind, I have at last broken free of the chains of fear that previously bound me. I have proved to myself that I am a person in control of my life and I am proud that this is so.

Helpful affirmations
- I can make a journey by plane whenever I wish.
- I am free of the fears that formerly bound me.
- I am proud of my ability to take control of my life.

8

Emotional Difficulties

It can be said that almost every problem arises because of some emotional difficulty, but what we will work on in this chapter are problems that arise because we don't really understand the way our emotions work or how to handle the situations that may arise.

RELATIONSHIPS

Say the word 'relationships' and most people will automatically think of situations between spouses or between long-term partners. But, of course, we have relationships with many people, beginning with our parents and going on to include schoolfriends, love affairs, work colleagues, children – plus all the other people who play significant roles in our lives. How we act in any kind of relationship depends a great deal on how we feel about ourselves. And that self-belief – whether good or bad – is usually created in the first few years of life. The attitude of parents, or those who act in that position, greatly affects the child and forms the basis for the way that child goes on to behave in their own relationships as an adult.

Case study: Tony
Tony was the only child of a couple that had married quite late – in fact his father was in his mid-50s when Tony was born. Although both parents loved him in their own way, his father

always seemed to Tony to be a distant and unapproachable figure. He certainly never showed any outward signs of the way he felt about Tony, tending to be somewhat strict and authoritarian. From a very early age Tony realized that the only way to get attention from his father was either to do something really bad – in which case the disapproval was made obvious, though he was never physically punished – or to excel in some way. So young Tony did everything he could to shine in some academic way as this appeared to give his father most pleasure and would even bring forth the occasional nod of approval and word of praise.

One day, when he was about seven years old, Tony rushed home from school to tell his father he had come top in the class spelling test and had only misspelled one word out of a hundred. He looked up at his father's face, waiting to see the half-smile and nod that would indicate his pleasure at this achievement. But his father frowned and said that if he could get 99 words right, he should have been able to spell all 100 correctly. And so life went on. Whatever he did, however hard he tried, Tony never seemed to gain his father's full approval.

Through a combination of hard work and natural ability, Tony went on to do very well at school and university. It was while he was still at university that his father died so he was never able to see the success Tony made of his career and working life – though not of his personal relationships. At 40 years old, Tony was still dissatisfied with his achievements. He ran his own successful business, he was financially well off, his future prospects were bright – but the strain of always trying to do better (to please that unappeasable father) brought him to the edge of emotional collapse.

Relationships with women had always been a disaster. If he found someone who assured him that she cared for him and respected him, Tony found himself unable to believe those words. He was more attracted to the type of woman who belittled him or showed contempt in some way, which was of course the path to pain. So he had never married or had the family he longed for. It was only after a complete emotional breakdown, requiring professional help from his doctor and from the hypnotherapist he consulted, that Tony was able to see what had led to his difficulties and to start to put his life together again.

Fitting the pattern

Why is it that someone like Tony – a pleasant, intelligent, hardworking person – cannot see himself for what he is? It is because his deep, inner opinion of himself was formed when very young – and it was formed by the attitude of his father and his own desperate attempts to please him. Because apparent disapproval appeared to be the norm, Tony grew up unable to believe that anyone who showed a different attitude to him could be telling the truth. The pattern did not fit with the one formed within him at his most impressionable age.

It is not unusual to hear of an attractive and intelligent woman who lurches from one disastrous love affair to another. All her friends can see she is drawn to the wrong type of man – but she is never aware of this until it is too late. In such cases, it is common to find that this woman, when a small girl, was made to feel that no one worthwhile would ever bother with her. Sometimes she might have been physically chastised, sometimes abused, sometimes just verbally belittled. Whatever the background, she will have been made to feel 'unworthy' or 'unlovable' in some way.

As the little girl grows up, because the pattern has to fit, she is drawn only to men who continue to make her feel this way. If someone comes along who adores her and puts her on a pedestal, she feels uncomfortable and cannot sustain the relationship. It's often difficult to break habitual patterns of behaviour: rather like if you have a parting in your hair, and one day decide to part it on the other side – for several days this will feel unnatural and uncomfortable. Think how much more uncomfortable and emotionally confusing it must feel to have someone treat you in a way that contradicts your own opinion of yourself. But should such a woman meet a man who, for example, belittles her, is violent towards her, has an alcohol problem or treats her badly in some other way, then the pattern fits. This emotional reaction ties in very well with the self-image she has grown up with and so, temporarily, she feels comfortable. It is only when the intelligent woman she has become realizes that this is no way to live her life that she will break such a relationship. But even then, she will probably accept that the blame for its failure is hers.

Be aware
No one goes through adolescence and into adult life without a few experiences of disastrous love affairs. But if you have gone on to be someone who goes through one emotional break-up after another – and if the pattern seems to be repeating itself – perhaps you need to take the time to look at your early life and see if some unfortunate pattern was set.

Forgiveness
Let's supposed you have managed to achieve this – with or without the help of a professional person – and you can now see who caused you to have this opinion of yourself, which draws you to people your inner self knows will continue the pattern. Hard as it may seem initially, the first thing you need to do is to forgive the person who is the cause of it all.

There are several ways of looking at this situation. In many cases, the person at the root of the problem may well have been someone who truly cared for you but, for whatever reason, was unable to show it in the way you needed. This could have been as a result of their own upbringing, in which case you could try to understand their problems and difficulties. Even if you feel this person knew full well what they were doing and was deliberately doing all they could to hurt you, that attitude must have come from something in their past and some hurt they suffered.

In either case, if you allow that person's effect on you to rule your life and govern your relationships, you are allowing them to continue to win – and I'm sure that isn't what you want. In addition, if you continue to be affected by them, you are more likely to pass these feelings on to your own children or to others you care for – and I don't believe you would want that either.

So you need to forgive that person from your past. It may be that they are no longer alive. It may be that they are still around but you know they are never going to change. If the latter is the case, you might well decide you want nothing more to do with them – but that doesn't mean you can't forgive them for something they may not have been able to help doing. If you have someone you need to forgive before you can get on with your own life in a positive way, the following script should be helpful (to be used, as ever, after the original induction script).

As I relax, I imagine myself in a very beautiful place, which I am creating in my own mind. It can be a place I know or I can simply imagine somewhere I know I would really like to be.

I walk around this place, looking to the right and to the left, taking in the beauty of the scene my mind has created. I am aware of all sensations. I can feel the warmth of the air on my skin, I can hear the sounds related to that place, I feel the texture of the ground beneath my feet.

This beautiful place extends far into the distance and I know that it is all mine, that I can come here whenever I wish and that I will always love it.

In my hand I am holding one end of a long piece of ribbon. The other end is so far away that I cannot see it. But I know it is being held by (insert name of person to be forgiven).

Each time I try to go forward to explore the distant parts of this beautiful place, I feel the ribbon jerk and I am pulled backward. I can only go so far and then the unseen hand on the far end of the ribbon holds me back.

For the first time I realize the solution lies in my own hand. The person holding the other end of the ribbon may be so much a victim of their own upbringing that they have no choice. But I know that I can choose whether or not I hold on to this ribbon.

To let it go and to go forwards happily to explore the rest of this beautiful place, all I have to do is to forgive with all my heart the person on the other end of the ribbon. Because I now understand that (name) is a victim in their own way, I am able to forgive them unconditionally for the way they acted towards me in the past.

As soon as I feel that unconditional forgiveness, the end of the ribbon slips from my hand and I leave it lying on the ground while I go forwards to explore the beauty that lies before me.

I am free of the past and of negative influences.

It is possible that using this script and doing this exercise may make you a little tearful, but don't worry – nothing is wrong. It simply means that at last you are experiencing the sensation of being your own person and of being able to go forward in the way you choose rather than as the victim of someone else's negativity. And that is a very big emotional step for anyone to take. If you do experience tears, they will soon pass and you will be filled with that sense of elation that accompanies your journey into a future of your own making.

Recognize the old pattern
Once you have managed to release yourself from the inner feelings brought with you from your past, you should find you respond differently within relationships, whichever type they may be. However, should you find yourself having further problems, stop and take an honest look at the other person, their attitude toward you and your reaction to them. If you become aware that the old pattern seems to be repeating itself, return to the script and work with it for a while longer.

Of course, in any type of relationship, you can only work on yourself. There is nothing you can do to change anyone else. Only they can do that for themselves – and they will only do so if they really want to. If, despite all the work you have done on yourself, the other person remains intransigent, you have to accept they are not going to change and you must either put up with the relationship as it is or walk away from it. But whichever decision you make, you will know you have made it from a position of awareness and understanding, and not because you cannot avoid following the old, unwanted path.

DEALING WITH BEREAVEMENT

The one thing we can be sure of in life is that, at some time or another, each of us is going to have to deal with the loss of someone we care about. Yet in the western world we tend to be ill prepared for this loss when it happens. Death is something rarely talked about and little advice is given on how to cope with it. Even when we know death comes as a release for someone who was enduring a life of suffering, we often find ourselves feeling guilty for daring to think such thoughts. It is important to realize there are three significant emotions that occur in almost everyone at a time of bereavement: sadness, anger and guilt. And we should be neither surprised nor worried to experience them all.

Sadness

This is probably the most expected reaction to death and is quite understandable. There is little that can be done – even if you wanted to – to avoid it but it can sometimes help to realize that, after a certain time, the sorrow we feel is predominantly for ourselves. Whatever your beliefs about what comes after this life, the person who has died is no longer suffering. If you believe that death is final and nothing exists beyond it, then they certainly cannot be experiencing grief or pain. If you believe that there is something more – even if you have no idea what that 'something' might be – then it is presumably a different type of existence to the one we understand. There can be no physical body, so there can be no pain.

So whatever type of death our loved suffered – instant or lingering – the sorrow we are experiencing is predominantly for ourselves and our loss. This is not selfishness; it is a warm, sincere feeling and, trite as it may sound, the only healer is time. The broadcaster David Jacobs, when talking about the loss of his wife in a tragic motor accident, once said, "You never get over it – but you do get used to it".

In addition, spiritualists and many others who believe in a life after death feel that you can actually impede the spiritual progress of the person who has died by clinging on to grief for too long. The essential being – whether you think of it as the 'spirit' or the 'soul' – is meant to go on through the various stages of afterlife in order to continue its journey. But if the person who has died is aware of intense grief and sorrow left behind on earth, they will not go on their way until they feel those left behind can cope.

Anger

Many people are surprised to find just how angry they feel when they have lost someone close to them. It could be that they are angry with that person for leaving them behind; they might just feel angry with the sun for shining. In my own case, when my husband died 20 years ago at a comparatively young age, I found myself looking at pensioners in the street, walking along arm in arm, and almost hating them for daring to grow old together when we would not have that to share. At the time this feeling of intense anger really worried me. Now, of course, I know it is a natural part of the grieving process and you simply have to accept this fact and know that eventually it will pass.

Guilt

This is the area where people often need most help. A sense of guilt almost always follows the death of someone close. It could be guilt for something said or not said, done or not done. It could be logical – such as never having had the opportunity to make up after an argument or tell them how much you really loved them. It could be illogical – as in the case of Eva.

Eva's husband, Dan, had been an insulin-dependent diabetic for several years. Doing her best to help him, Eva had carefully controlled his diet according to the advice she had been given. One of Dan's pleasures, particularly in the summer, was the glass of diabetic beer he was allowed in the evening. The days leading up to Dan's death had been very hot and sultry, and the night before his fatal heart attack, having drunk his usual glass of beer, Dan had told his wife that he fancied another beer. Having her husband's best interests at heart, Eva had refused because this would alter his blood sugar level, which they were so carefully monitoring.

When Dan sadly died the following morning, Eva was distraught. Theirs had been a true love affair for more than 30 years and they had frequently told each other of their feelings. Having nothing to reproach herself for, Eva's mind latched on to the fact she had refused Dan that extra glass of beer the previous evening. She felt so guilty at having done so when now he was not there to enjoy one at all. Of course, if she had given him the beer and he had died the next day, Eva would probably have felt guilty for giving it to him and might even have wondered if it had contributed to his death.

Unfinished business

The type of guilt experienced by Eva is perfectly natural and will pass with time. But sometimes the guilt experienced is centred far more in fact. It may be a feeling of guilt for not having been there to say goodbye, for not having communicated with that person for too long, for never having told them how much you loved them, or perhaps for having wronged them in some way.

The following script is designed to help you complete such 'unfinished business' with the person who has died. They will hear you, they will understand, and they will forgive. People don't stop loving you just because they are dead. And, whatever that other life may be like, their wisdom will have increased rather than decreased – which will make their love, understanding and forgiveness even easier.

During the script you will need to picture the person who has died. Remember you can picture them at whatever period in their life you choose – it does not have to be how they looked toward the end if this is something you would find distressing.

As I relax now I allow thoughts of (name) to come into my mind. I see him/her at whatever age and whatever stage of life I choose – the way I most want to remember him/her.

For a few moments, as we come together, I send thoughts of love to him/her and I am aware of a deep love being returned to me. For both of us this is a non-critical and unquestioning love, a love that transcends the physical and has no boundaries.

I acknowledge to (name) that I have feelings of guilt because (insert reason). Because it is now too late to make amends on an earthly level, I wish to do so on a spiritual level, and to do so I need their love and co-operation.

Now take the time to explain in detail, in your own words, all the reasons you may have for your feelings of guilt.

Because I know that (name) is now in a place of deeper understanding and forgiveness, I await the answer I know he/she wants to give.

Remain silent now and allow that answer to come into your mind, holding on to the image you have of the deceased person. If you feel they have wronged you in any way during their lifetime, ask for an explanation of how this arose, using something like: *I feel there remains an unresolved situation between us and I have a need to understand what happened, and the reasons for it.*

Now go on to put into your own words the situation concerned and ask for an explanation. Then remain silent and, once again, allow the answer to come freely into your mind.

I give my thanks to the spirit of (name) for helping me put to rest any unfinished business between us, and I am able to forgive both him/her and myself for any part we played in our mutual misunderstanding.

I send my love to (name) and hope that his/her spiritual journey will be one of peace, joy and love.

Other people

One of the hardest things for a newly bereaved person to deal with – and sometimes one of the hardest to understand – is the reaction of some other people. Some people will come close, offer what comfort they can, and be as supportive as possible – yet even they may feel awkward or find it difficult to know what to say. Others will stay away, fail to mention the subject and even appear to go out of their way to avoid you. None of this is intended to be hurtful or disrespectful. All it means is that people are often uncomfortable with death and bereavement, and feel embarrassed because they do not know what are the right things to say or do – so they try to get out of saying and doing anything.

Try not to allow yourself to be hurt by this reaction from others around you. Of course it is wrong when what you really need is the presence of people who care about you, whether they say the 'right' thing or not. Try instead to understand their awkwardness as a sign that they do not want to cause you further pain. You may find it helpful to create a script based on the forgiveness aspect mentioned earlier in this chapter.

GENERAL FEELINGS OF GUILT

Leaving aside the guilt associated with bereavement, most of us feel guilty about something in our lives. Sometimes this is because of some deliberate wrong we have done, sometimes it is because of words we wish we had not said or things we wish we had not done. Many people try to bury the guilt deep within themselves and go on with their lives as if the sins of omission or commission had never occurred. But this simply does not work. Left to its own devices, guilt will fester inside you and can infect the rest of your life. The only thing to do, if you have these feelings of guilt, is to bring them to the fore, look at them, understand them, deal with them – then let them go forever.

Let's suppose for a moment that, at some time in the past, you did or said something that you know was wrong or that caused distress to another person. If there is any way in which the words or actions can be put right and an apology or explanation given, this will obviously be a sensible and therapeutic move on your part. Sometimes this is not possible. Perhaps the other person is no longer around or the deed cannot be repaired. In such cases, holding on to guilt can achieve no good and can in fact damage the remainder of your life. The only steps you can take are to acknowledge to yourself that you were wrong, vow that you will not repeat the mistake, and try to learn from the experience.

There is no such thing as a perfect person. There is no human being that has not done something they regret in the past. But just as you would do your best to understand and forgive the errors of someone else, it is important to grant yourself the same privilege.

Dealing with guilt
If you suffer from a sense of guilt for anything in your past, here

are some steps and a script to help you deal with the situation in a such a way that you are able to live your life to the full again.

1. Acknowledge to yourself what you have done and how it makes you feel about yourself. (Sometimes it can help to write down such thoughts.) Maybe what you did was accidental and unintentional hurt was caused to someone else, in which case the guilt can be just as severe.

2. Have you done whatever you can to put matters right? Sometimes this is possible and sometimes it is not. If you have caused physical injury to somebody else by your carelessness, for example, you cannot 'undo' that injury. Where possible, try to put things right and, where that is not possible, see if you can apologize to the person or people concerned. If that person refuses to listen, or if they are no longer around, try to make reparation in some other way – perhaps by giving your time and energy to help someone else.

3. Learn from what you did. Only you can know how much pain you have inflicted upon yourself as a result of your words or actions (or lack of them). So only you can make a firm decision to attempt never to repeat the mistake. Once you have done this, no useful purpose can be served by clinging on to the feelings of guilt and the feelings of self-disgust that often accompany them. If you are to live a complete and fulfilling life and be of benefit to yourself and others, you have to let those feelings go.

Guilt script

As I relax, I imagine myself on a beautiful sandy beach. It is a lovely day. The sun is shining in a blue, blue sky and there is enough of a gentle breeze to prevent the heat being too intense. I can hear the birds calling overhead and the sound of the waves lapping on the shore.

I am walking along the beach and I should be enjoying it but I am hampered by a heavy weight attached to my ankle by a strong rope. This weight is so great that it makes walking difficult so that my progress along the sand is slow and laboured.

I know this weight symbolizes the guilt I have been feeling and the negative thoughts this has caused me to have about myself as a person. In the past, I have always believed I deserved to have these feelings but now I realize that, having made all the reparation I can and having learned a lesson from my mistake, I am allowed to dispense with the weight and to set myself free from the guilt.

I sit down on the firm sand at the water's edge and feel the small waves lapping over my feet – but the weight is still firmly attached and I do not know how to remove it.

Using my finger, I write in the damp sand these words: 'I forgive myself unconditionally for (insert error)'. As I watch, one wave comes slightly further in on the sand and washes over my words, drawing them back into the ever-moving sea. I realize this acceptance of my words of forgiveness by the sea is a sign that they have been accepted.

Another wave comes up on to the shore and, as I look at it, I see it has washed on to the sand a sharp stone of pure white. I use this stone to cut through the rope attaching the heavy weight to my ankle.

Now I am free. I rise to my feet and start to walk freely along the sandy shore. Freedom from the weight I have been carrying for so long is exhilarating and I begin to run, enjoying the sensation of the sun on my body and the warm sand beneath my feet.

I know that, by taking these actions, I have freed myself for ever from the burden of guilt that has been holding me back and I can go forward with hope, and live the rest of my life as it should be lived.

Helpful affirmations
- I have released myself from the burden of guilt.
- I forgive myself for my past errors.
- I am free to live my life as I wish.

Case study: Martin
Martin was not a wicked young man – but he was a weak one. When he was 19 years old and a student he had a vacation job working for a friend of his father. One of his duties was to keep the accounts, invoices and receipts up to date so that the accountant could deal with them.

At that time Martin had a new girlfriend and, like many young men, he was anxious to impress her and to take her to the places she wanted to go. Unfortunately his income was not sufficient to do that and, rather than admit his lack of money, he succumbed to temptation and altered some of the figures in the books, enabling himself to 'borrow' extra funds from his boss. He knew what he was doing was wrong but convinced himself that he would put the money back in the near future.

Inevitably Martin's deception was discovered and he was immediately sacked from the job. His father repaid the stolen money to his friend who agreed, for the sake of their friendship, not to press charges. Not only did Martin lose his girlfriend when she found out what he had been doing, but Martin was well aware of how much he had hurt his father and let down his family. He had also caused a rift between his father and his former employer as their mutual embarrassment about what had occurred made their friendship difficult.

In the years that followed, although Martin never did anything like it again, his guilt never left him. He tried to keep it buried but his sense of self-dislike grew until it affected many areas of his life. He always felt that his family were judging him and waiting for him to do something similar again. He was awkward about friendships and relationships because his inner image was of someone who was not worthy of liking and trust, and he was always afraid other people would discover his shameful secret.

It was only when he reached his late 30s and was depressed about the break-up of yet another relationship that he decided something had to be done about his sense of guilt and he consulted a local counsellor. Martin was asked whether he had made financial reparation to his father who had refunded the money to his former employer. This he had done many years before, but it had done little to improve his opinion of himself. He was asked if he had apologized for his actions and he said that he had, though he did not feel that such an apology was sufficient for the way in which he had let everybody down. He was asked if he had learned anything from his mistake and he replied that he supposed he had because he had never been tempted to do anything similar again. He was asked whether he had forgiven himself for his misdeed and he replied he could not because, when he remembered his mother's tears and the look in his father's eyes, he felt he did not deserve to be forgiven. He was then asked whether his continued refusal to forgive himself was serving any useful purpose. After some thought, Martin realized it was not. He was not by nature dishonest and he knew that, whether or not he let go of his guilt, he would never be tempted to steal again. So Martin and the counsellor worked on achieving this sense of self-forgiveness and, though it took some time for the feelings of guilt to disappear, eventually Martin was able to face the future with a positive outlook.

9

Performance under Pressure

This chapter, and the scripts it contains, are designed to help you perform effectively during those moments when you are required to give of your best. It will help you to deal with such things as tests and exams, interviews, sporting events and drama performances, enabling you to give the best performance you are capable of giving.

If you think about those, often terrifying, occasions such as driving tests, job interviews or examinations, you will realize that when we do badly it is usually because we are suffering from nerves rather than because we actually lack ability. Self-hypnosis alone cannot guarantee you will pass your driving test if you do not know how to do an emergency stop; it will not get you through an exam with flying colours if you haven't done any revision; and it won't ensure you are offered that longed-for job if there is another person more suitably qualified. What it will do is make sure that you do not let yourself down in any such situation simply because your nervousness is so great that you cannot think or act in the best way possible. Whatever the final result, you will be able to come away from the situation knowing you did the very best you were able to do and that you did not let yourself down in any way.

SPORT

This is one area where attitude and outlook can make all

the difference. I am sure you will have seen the look on the face of certain athletes, such as champion sprinter Linford Christie, at the beginning of a contest. That look says 'I am fully prepared. I am positive. I am confident that, no matter what, I am about to give my very best performance.' You too can adopt that look of determination.

If you are a player of team sport, you can almost guarantee that team will win its next game or match if each member is hypnotized in advance. This is because in any team – regardless of the number of members – one person will have had a bad night's sleep; another may have had an argument with a husband, wife or partner; yet another may have toothache. It is extremely rare for every single member of a team to be playing to the very best of their ability. But should each member of that team have worked through self-hypnosis to fulfil their full potential, a win is very likely.

When it comes to an individual competitor, however, the odds may be different. A runner, for example, may enter a race where another competitor happens to be physically stronger or faster and therefore turns out to be the winner. What you can be sure of, however, is that our individual runner will give the best performance of their lifetime.

Teams in countries such as the United States and the former Soviet Union have had what they call 'psychological coaches' for a number of years. Many of these sports psychologists are in fact qualified hypnotherapists who have chosen to apply their expertise in this particular field. That trend is now spreading throughout Europe, even reaching the shores of the UK, and where it has been in use the results have been clearly and satisfyingly visible.

Let's suppose you are involved in a particular sport. You have been playing for some time and are reasonably adept at the technical skills required. How are you going to give yourself that extra edge, which turns you from an enthusiastic player into a person who is respected and recognized as being particularly skilful in that sport? The answer is you need a role model or a mentor – someone who is already at the top in your specific sport. I don't know anything about you or the sport that interests you but I am certain you can think of someone famous and successful in the world of that sport; your hero or heroine – someone who plays in exactly the type of way you wish you could play. You may never meet that person in real life but they are going to help you to improve your prowess.

The following script can become as important to you as your regular physical practice in your chosen sport.

As I relax, I know I am preparing myself mentally and emotionally for the next time I take part in (name of sport). I also know that this positive mental attitude, when combined with existing physical ability, will give me a particularly good advantage on the next sporting occasion. It will enable me to give my best performance ever and to feel really pleased with the way I have been performing.

There is one person who plays my chosen sport in precisely the way I would like to play it and that is (insert name). And I am going to enlist the aid of that person in order to improve my own performance.

In my mind now, I imagine myself preparing for a performance or a contest. I see the picture in my head, exactly as it will be when the actual day arrives. The only difference is that, where I am waiting to begin, I imagine the head and body of (mentor) superimposed over my own.

As I allow this scene to progress in my mind, observing the process as it normally takes place, each time I am participating I still imagine that superimposed head and body over mine, so that the performance is that of (mentor).

I know that, provided I work regularly with this image while also keeping up my physical practice sessions, when the time comes for me to show what I can do, I will perform exactly as (mentor) performs within the limits of my own physical ability. I will play the best I have played in my life and I will be extremely proud of my performance.

Although (name of mentor) is not aware that he/she is helping me in this way, nonetheless I send them my thanks for their assistance and I am confident that, thanks to my reinforced positive attitude, I will play in such a way that he/she would be proud of me.

I can assure you that, over the years, this method has been used with teams and individuals with great success. Indeed, we used it with more than 50 football teams – always the 'underdog', as there is nothing clever about helping the one who was likely to win anyway – and on every occasion those teams won, whatever the prediction.

JOB INTERVIEWS

You can adapt the sports script to help you with any job interviews you might have in the future. In this case your mentor is unlikely to be anyone famous but you should choose someone who acts and speaks with the type of confidence you would like to display when the interview takes place.

Naturally you will have to do your homework before the interview. You need to know something about the company you are approaching and to be sure that you have the skills and aptitudes it is seeking. Self-hypnosis will not do that for you. What it will do, however, is eradicate the usual panic and nervousness, which causes most people to let themselves down at interviews.

Perhaps someone else will attend the interview that is far more qualified than you – and perhaps that person will be offered the job you were hoping for. But even if that occurs, you will be certain you acquitted yourself well and that there is nothing more you could have done. You will avoid the usual self-doubt and personal post mortem, where you ask yourself whether there is something you could have done differently to make yourself appear more suitable for the position. This will enable you to come away from the situation with your confidence and self-esteem intact – which in turn will help you to do just as well at any subsequent interview that might arise.

DRIVING TEST

More driving tests are failed because of 'nerves' than for any other reason. We have all known people who have taken their test many, many times and failed it, even though we know they are competent drivers.

Case study: Louise

Louise had never bothered to take her driving test as a young woman because she had always lived close to efficient public transport and it had never seemed to be necessary. When she married she stayed in the same area and if she and her partner wanted to go out for an evening, when less transport was available, her husband would drive. But the time came when Louise found herself the mother of two young boys and experienced the difficulties of trying to take children, pushchair and shopping basket on and off local buses and trains. So she decided the time had come to take driving lessons.

Her driving instructor was very pleased with her progress and, when he thought she was ready, he suggested she apply for a test date. He was quite convinced she would pass the test at the first opportunity. When the day arrived Louise was so nervous, she was over-cautious on the test and also made some silly mistakes when performing required manoeuvres. She failed. After that she took her test with monotonous regularity and the situation was always the same. When she went out with her driving instructor or friends, who felt confident enough to accompany her as her 'experienced driver', Louise would drive perfectly well. But as soon as the test day arrived, she would become so nervous that she would make silly mistakes and let herself down again.

How long this situation would have continued is uncertain, but the day before her seventh driving test Louise was told her father had suffered a mild heart attack from which he was expected to make a full recovery. Concern about her father's condition pushed all fears out of Louise's mind and she showed no sign of nerves as she sat in the car and prepared for her test. She passed.

I am not suggesting you wait until you experience some family worry before taking your driving test. What I am trying to show is that if you release your mind from those crippling attacks of nerves, you are likely to perform well. The way to achieve this by means of self-hypnosis is to use the induction script and then, always re-emphasising how relaxed you are feeling, to imagine the driving test as it will be on the day. Visualize the whole thing, from checking door and mirrors right through to the time when the examiner tells you that you have passed. See yourself doing everything exactly as you know it should be done – and doing it in a calm, controlled and confident manner.

Repeat this process for at least three weeks prior to the date of your driving test and, provided you know how to handle a car, you will eliminate those crippling nerves that might otherwise occur.

Helpful affirmations
• I am a good and competent driver.
• I drive a car with confidence and self-assurance.
• I deserve to pass my driving test.

PASSING EXAMS

If you wish to pass your exams, there are three things to look at – and self-hypnosis can help with all of them.

The first aspect for consideration is how you keep a record of what you have studied and what you need to know. In many cases, students of all ages have a tendency to be far too long-winded in their notes and therefore make it much more difficult for themselves when it comes to revision time. There is so much paperwork to get through that, not only does it appear daunting, it takes a great deal of time and effort.

Keywords
These are important, whatever topic you happen to be studying. Think of any book, any essay, any lecture and you will realize that the relevant and important words and phrases have to be cushioned in a mass of 'ordinary' words so that they make sense. But 'and', 'then' and 'later' are not necessary when it comes to revision. If you were to go to any single page of a book, which happens to be relevant to your studies, it is probable that there are no more than ten to fifteen significant words or phrases (keywords)

that would give you all the information contained on that page. Commit these keywords to memory and when it comes to reproducing the information on the page, you can supply your own linking words and repeat the facts in your own way.

So the first stage is to go through any texts, lecture notes or essays you may have and pick out those keywords and write them down. Although it is not essential to use self-hypnosis to do this, you will find it much easier if you first relax yourself by using the initial induction and relaxation technique given at the beginning of the book.

Don't try to work for too many hours at a time. Some people consider they must revise for several hours a day without a break but this is definitely counter-productive for two reasons:

Experts have shown that the human brain is able to absorb most information when the effort made is broken down into periods of approximately seventy-five minutes. To go on much longer will mean that each additional piece of information takes more time to absorb.

It has also been shown that we absorb best and remember almost anything we study at the beginning and end of a session. It is therefore better to have several sessions of an hour or so (thereby having several beginnings and several endings) than to study for an entire day.

When it comes to committing those keywords to memory, self-hypnosis can definitely play its part in the following way. (As always, use this script after the initial induction script given earlier).

I am relaxed and comfortable, and because I am breathing slowly and easily, oxygen reaches my brain more effectively. This improves the functioning of my brain and makes it easier for me to learn whatever I wish.

I have converted all or part of what I need to know into the relevant keywords and now I am going to commit those keywords to memory.

Feeling completely relaxed, I visualize in front of me a large white board on the wall. Beside it are several thick black marker pens ready for use.

I take the first list of keywords I have to study and, maintaining deep relaxation, I open my eyes and read slowly down the list.

Closing my eyes again, I imagine each of those words being written, one at a time, on that white board by an invisible hand holding one of the thick, black marker pens. It is important that the words are written slowly in capital letters and one letter at a time.

This is not a test or an examination and should I reach a point where I am unable to recall the next keyword, I can open my eyes and look at my written list before closing them again and allowing the invisible hand holding the pen to continue its work.

When my first list has been completed and all the words are there before me on that imaginary white board, I read them slowly, one at a time, in order to fix them in my long-term memory.

Repeat this exercise several times until you are able to imagine that hand writing each word in turn without having to open your eyes to check your list. Then proceed as follows:

Those keywords are now fixed in my memory and I can recall them whenever I want. I know that, by recalling those words, I will be able to reproduce the information in the original text in such a way that I can make clear what I have learned.

I will therefore have sufficient knowledge to pass the test or examination that confronts me. The additional confidence this fact gives me will also be helpful when it comes to the day of the examination.

You can repeat the above script with each set of keywords you have selected but do not be tempted to go on to the second list until you are positive you have fully absorbed list one, or you may find yourself becoming confused. Provided there are no more than about fifteen keywords in your list, you should find you can absorb those words in a single session of self-hypnosis (though, as indicated in the script, you may have to repeat them two or three times within that session).

The examination
As with driving tests and job interviews, more people fail to do as well as they should in exams because of nerves than because they

do not have the required knowledge. Some say that this is sufficient reason for abolishing exams and tests, but life is full of testing situations and learning to cope with them in the right way can be beneficial throughout life, not just at exam time.

When it comes to formal examinations, it is best to begin preparing yourself a few weeks in advance. Even a single session of the relevant self-hypnosis will be helpful but a full preparation period will enable your subconscious mind to be fully convinced you are going to remain calm and acquit yourself well.

The place of examination
For many people the place of the exam will be quite familiar – perhaps their normal school, college or workplace. Others may have to go to some unknown environment in order to take a specific exam. If at all possible, try and find out precisely what the place looks like. If for some reason this is not possible – perhaps because it is too far from home or because it is somewhere you are not permitted to enter – don't panic. Most exam rooms have the same sort of layout. They are likely to be quite large, with a number of desks or tables set out in rows, and there will be one table or desk in the room that is for the invigilator.

However well you prepare, there are bound to be some nerves on the day itself. This is not a bad thing, provided your nervousness is kept to a minimum, as it will cause the adrenaline to flow and help you to think quickly. Either extreme, however, is detrimental. If your nerves are so bad that they almost cause you to panic, you will not be able to think clearly. Your mind may even appear to go blank and you will become very stressed and tense. If you are too laid back, you may not put enough effort into your exam and may fail to do yourself justice as a result. The following script should help you to achieve the correct balance.

I am feeling very relaxed and very comfortable. Because this is truly important at this time, I spend a few extra moments concentrating on the steadiness of my breathing and on the fact that my shoulders are relaxed, as are the muscles in my jaw. I can feel myself growing ever more relaxed... more relaxed... more relaxed... as I concentrate on the steady rhythm of my breathing. As I proceed with the following visualization, I shall remember at all times to be aware of that feeling of deep and pleasant relaxation.

In my mind now I visualize the room in which the examination is to be taken. If I have never seen the actual room in reality, I just have to visualize a typical scene and I will be perfectly at ease.

I imagine myself sitting at one of the desks or tables in that room (it does not matter if I do not know the precise one I shall be using). As I sit there, I reinforce the feelings of relaxation by concentrating on my shoulders, my jaw and my slow and regular breathing.

The examination paper is face down on the desk in front of me, and as I look at it I become ever more relaxed, knowing I have prepared well and I am about to do my best.

Now it is time to turn over the paper. I do so but, before even picking up my pen, I spend a few moments concentrating on my breathing, ensuring I am breathing deeply and well.

I pick up my pen and start to work through the questions on the examination paper. I work steadily, answering the questions to the best of my ability.

If at any point I begin to feel uneasy about the examination paper or any of the questions on it, I stop for a moment to ensure I am fully relaxed – that my shoulders are relaxed, my forehead is clear and my jaw is relaxed too. I take two or three really deep breaths and continue to answer the questions on the paper.

When the time comes for the examination to end, I put down my pen and take three very deep breaths, knowing I have done the best I can and have answered all the questions to the best of my ability.

Helpful affirmations
- I can relax when taking examinations.
- The more I relax, the better I can reproduce what I know.
- I will remain calm throughout.

Help yourself
There are various other ways in which you can help yourself before, during and after the examination:
- If you are among a group of people that have to take the same

examination, try to avoid too much advance contact with those who have a tendency to panic. Agitation and panic are catching and, should you let it affect you, you will find it harder to calm down again when the exam itself is due.

- Similarly, once the examination is over, keep away from those people who have a tendency to hold their heads and claim they know they have failed. Whether this is true or not, nothing can be done to change things now but you will make yourself feel uneasy and cause yourself distress for nothing.
- It makes sense to look after your health and well-being in the run-up to any time that could prove stressful. Whatever your normal habits, try to ensure you get sufficient vitamins and minerals, either in your diet or by means of supplements. The right amount of sleep is also beneficial and, even more so, the right *quality* of sleep. Here, too, you can use one of the self-hypnosis scripts to help you.

You may not be an avid fan of physical exercise but a short, brisk walk each day in the period before an exam can make you feel better and will increase the amount of oxygen to the brain. This will improve your performance, both when studying and on the day of the exam itself. Don't be tempted to overdo things and run yourself into exhaustion. You need to do just enough to get the circulation going and the mind working clearly.

Put together all the points mentioned plus the scripts for learning and sitting the examination and, even if you don't end up top of the class, you are bound to do better than you ever have before, and will feel proud of yourself and confident in your own abilities.

Case study: Tony

As part of their career advancement in the civil service, Tony and several colleagues had to take a series of tests and exams. One of these was an exam in accounting– which had never been Tony's best subject. Tony worked hard for his exams and also used self-hypnosis throughout, which helped him a great deal. However, once the exam itself was over, he went for a drink and post mortem with his colleagues. They began to discuss a particular question that each of them had found difficult. 'What answer did you arrive at?' asked one colleague, uttering with a sigh of relief, 'Oh, good, that was my answer too' when he heard the reply.

Tony said nothing but inwardly he began to panic, particularly when one or two others agreed with the answer given. He had not reached the same conclusion as those other people – what had he done wrong? Although he realized that, right or wrong, there was nothing he could do to change his answers, Tony became very stressed and anxious over the following few weeks, convincing himself he must have done so badly in the exam that he had probably ruined his future prospects. When the results came through, Tony found that not only had he passed the exam with flying colours but that he was one of only five people to arrive at the correct solution to the problem they had all been discussing. So all those sleepless nights and anxious days had been for nothing.

Whether you have done as well as you should in your own examination, you can still cause yourself tension while you wait for the results to become available if you take part in too many post mortems. It is over – you have done your best. You might just as well put it from your mind until the true results are given.

10

Making Your Future

Whatever has happened in your life up to this moment, whatever the problems you may have had, however difficult the people or situations you have had to deal with, from this moment on it is up to you. You are now in a position to select and make a success of your own future.

Hopefully, as you have read this book, you have been able to deal successfully with any problems that may have resulted from your past, so that you are now able to go forward and work towards your future. If you have not done this yet, please pause here and work on any aspect of yourself that requires it before proceeding with the techniques set out in this chapter.

You will have discovered by now the great power of your subconscious mind. It is all-knowing – it understands you far better than conscious thought alone can ever do. It is the seat of your emotions and of your intuitive self, and it is the latter that you can use to plan for the future. Whatever stage you have reached in your life – whether you are young or old – you have arrived at a truly exciting moment. This is the time when you are going to make choices and plans that will influence the whole of the rest of your life. Whether these plans can be achieved quickly, or whether circumstances mean they take a little longer to come to fruition, is unimportant. This is the moment when you will know you are truly in control of your own life and your own destiny.

As you read this chapter, you will fall into one of two main categories. Some of you will have a very clear idea of what you would like to do in the future, even if you are not yet certain how

to go about it; others will know they are seeking some sort of ful-
filment but will not even know what it is or how they are to
achieve it. If you fall into the latter category, you may need to give
your subconscious mind a little prod – a little extra help in showing you what it wants you to know. If this applies to you, start by
making lists of:

- your likes and dislikes about the way your life is now and has
  been in the past;
- your (perhaps secret) hopes and fears for the future;
- your current skills and aptitudes, as well as any you might be
  interested in enhancing in the future;
- your commitments and anything that might affect what you
  are able to do during the next phase of your life.

When your lists have been completed – and I would recommend writing them over the course of a few days rather than all
at once – read them through several times. Now, adapting that
original script for relaxation in any way you please, take yourself
to a special secret place in the centre of your mind. Relax as
deeply as you are able to and allow your mind to drift however it
wishes around the thoughts you have had. Don't try to guide
your thoughts too much or to force them to go in a particular
direction. Imagine you are watching a film unfold inside your
head and that, like any audience, you are waiting to see how the
film will end. An ideal time to practise this is in bed, just before
allowing yourself to drift off to sleep. This will give your subconscious mind time to work during the night when your conscious
mind has shut down and you are asleep.

Don't worry if you do not seem to experience any results for a
while; it may be that your subconscious is not used to being given
the freedom to work in such a way. Persevere and you will find –
as great thinkers such as Edison, Shakespeare and Einstein have
found – that one morning you will wake up to find the answer has
been given to you. You will know for certain what it is that you
want to achieve and in which direction you wish to proceed. Then
it will be up to you to work out the practicalities of how you are
going to go about it.

Case study: Sarah

Sarah had taken early retirement from her work in the offices of a large insurance company. She had not enjoyed her job particularly, though she was extremely efficient and had become supervisor of her department. But as a single mother with three daughters to bring up, she had been happy to find a job that she could do with ease and that paid sufficiently well for her to care for her family.

Once the girls had grown up and left home, Sarah was only too pleased when the opportunity arose for early retirement and she gratefully took advantage of the situation. Her pension and the fact that she now had only herself to look after meant that, though she was by no means rich, she did not have any real financial worries. But Sarah knew she was not the sort of person who would be happy just to sit at home and do nothing; the question was, how was she to decide how she wanted to spend her time in the future?

Sarah began by making her lists. She knew she was an extremely practical person, able to run an office efficiently. She knew she seemed able to get on very well with other people – she was a 'people person' who would not be happy spending all her time on her own. She also knew she had a great love of animals but had been discouraged early in her life from doing anything about this, first by her ever-practical parents who decided that the best thing for any young woman was to become efficient in office skills, and later by her need to earn a reasonable salary in order to support her young family. The only way in which Sarah had been able to indulge this love of animals was by having a couple of cats as pets and allowing her daughters, as they grew up, to have the usual assortment of hamsters, gerbils, rabbits and guinea pigs.

Allowing her subconscious mind and her intuition to take over, Sarah decided that the time had come when she could do more in the way of caring for animals. But she had no qualifications for this and no particular knowledge of how to care for them, other than the usual pet owner's experience. What was she to do?

Suddenly an opportunity presented itself. For some years Sarah had done what she could to help a local animal sanctuary – giving a little money when she could afford it and giving her time

when it came to running jumble sales and garden fetes in order
help raise funds. In the latest newsletter, the head of the sanctuary
asked whether anyone would be willing to give some time and
help in their office, answering telephone enquiries, dealing with
paperwork and with members of the public. If someone could be
found to help out in this way, it would release other members of
staff who had the necessary skills to work with the animals
themselves.

Sarah decided this job was for her and she approached the
head of the sanctuary, who was delighted to accept her offer.
Accustomed as she was to office routines, Sarah found the work
very easy and really enjoyed dealing with the public, particularly
those who were keen to adopt one or more of the animals being
cared for. Seeing how desperate the charity-reliant sanctuary was
for aid, Sarah began to spend some time helping with the feeding
of domestic animals and even started walking some of the aban-
doned dogs, which otherwise would not have had sufficient exercise. She began to feel really happy and fulfilled. The sanctuary
owners were grateful for her practical help and Sarah was able to
spend time with the animals she loved.

MAKING CHOICES

Sometimes you might be undecided about more than one possible
future direction and find it difficult to decide which would be the
best for you. Here, too, self-hypnosis can help.

Suppose, for example, you have a decision to make about
which of two possible directions would be better for you. Using
the relaxation induction script, relax as deeply as possible. Then,
in your mind, take yourself into a peaceful room where, in addition to your favourite furniture and decor, there is a large television set, a video recorder and a shelf full of video cassettes, all of
which relate to you and your life.

In your imagination select one of these video cassettes, insert it
in the machine, sit back and watch the screen. Watch as the 'film'
unfolds, showing you your future if you were to follow one of the

directions you have been contemplating. Don't try to force the image or to use logic to 'make' an outcome occur – just relax and see what appears. If there is nothing much, try again later or even the following day.

When your subconscious mind has presented you with the future scenario if you were to follow one path, select the other cassette – the one that will show you the likely outcome if you were to follow a different path. Repeat the process, as with the first video (always remembering the relaxation technique first) and allow your subconscious to show you what is likely to happen in the second case.

When you have 'seen' the probable result of following each of the possible paths to your future, you should have a far better idea of which is likely to prove better for you. If, at that point, you can honestly say there appears to be no difference in the benefits that will come to you, all you need to do is choose the one that appeals to you the most.

CONFIDENCE/SELF-ESTEEM

Once your desired goal has become clear to you and you have decided to aim for it, the thing that is most likely to stand in your way is your own self-doubt about whether you will be able to achieve what you want. This is quite natural, particularly if the goal is something that is really important to you. Most of us have a tendency to feel we would be taking on too much or even that we are not 'good enough' to reach our goals. This is not true. If you have something you really want to achieve and if you are prepared to work for it, you can do it. Don't allow self-doubt to get in your way and spoil your future. There are three stages to using self-hypnosis to convince yourself that you have what it takes to achieve your aims.

1. Consider the past
I would like you to pause for a moment and think of a time in your past (from your earliest childhood onward) when you felt

really proud of yourself. Before you rush to say that you can't
think of such a moment, stop. Everyone, whatever their background, has such a moment. Even if you have never won a prize,
or come top in some selection, perhaps you can remember the day
you first managed to ride a bicycle without the need for stabiliz-
ers or a steadying hand. What about the time you first managed
to swim a width in the swimming pool without having to put a
foot on the ground? If you are able to drive, surely you can recall
that feeling when at last you were able to tear up those hated L-
plates? The event does not have to be great in world terms or even
something everyone knew about – just a moment in time when
you experienced what I call the 'wow' factor. When you felt excited, happy, proud or exhilarated because you had achieved something you really wanted to do.

Once you have found your 'wow' moment, pause and remember exactly how it made you feel. Did you feel like laughing or
crying for joy? Did you feel the excitement in your head or perhaps in your stomach? Did you shake or want to shout your
achievement out loud? We all react differently to such moments
and it is important to understand yourself and your personal
response to 'wow'.

2. Visualize your future goal
Whatever it is you have decided you *want* to achieve (not *hope* to
achieve – doubt does not figure in this visualization), turn it into
a picture.

As with any visualization, it is important to make this picture
as clear and as positive as possible. Work on it until you can see it
in great detail, just as you would like it to be. Don't worry if the
exact place where it will all happen is unknown to you at the present time. If you want to learn to ski, one mountainside is pretty
much like any other for this purpose. If your aim is to travel to,
say, India, a few travel books will give you a pretty good idea of
what to expect. If you have ambitions to become a writer, the precise style of your desk or make of your computer is unimportant.
What is important is that you are able to see yourself fulfilling this
ambition and know that, in your visualization, you have already

attained your goal. Once you have perfected this image, you are ready to move on to the third stage.

3. The script

Because there are likely to be as many ambitions as there are readers of this book, not to mention as many 'wow' moments, I am going to use an imaginary example for the purposes of this script. When you come to adapt it for your own use, naturally you will substitute your own exciting moment and goal for the one provided.

I am going to suppose we are dealing with a woman called June. When she was young, June studied for a law degree and after completing her articles qualified as a solicitor. But, having reached that stage, she married and almost immediately became pregnant. She and her husband went on to have four children and, finances not being a great problem, June decided she wanted to be at home with her children while they were young. As the children grew older and went to school, June still wanted to be there for them during the holidays, so she worked for an agency as a 'temp' in various offices, as and when she was needed.

When the children finally left home to go to university or to follow their own paths, June decided she would really like to work as a solicitor, following her original training. She appreciated there would be a considerable amount of catching up to do as many things had obviously changed over the years, but this did not really worry her. Studying and exams had never really been a problem. What did concern her was her own self-doubt about the responsibility she would be undertaking and whether she would be able, first, to get the kind of position she would like and, second, to acquit herself well within that position.

Let's suppose that June's 'wow' moment was when, after overcoming her nerves, she was able to dive from the top board at the swimming pool. She will always remember how, having done it once, she could not wait to do it again and again, and how the thrill of the achievement had caused her pulse to race and made her want to laugh out loud. Now recalling this moment will help her to achieve her new goal.

As I lie here, deeply, deeply relaxed, I remember the time when I first managed to dive from the highest board at the swimming pool. I can recall the sensation of what felt like flying through the air, the exhilaration of making a perfect entry into the water beneath, and the absolute joy as my head cleared the water again and I realized I had done it!

I climbed out of the water and was aware that my pulse was racing with sheer excitement and joy, and that I wanted to laugh and shout with the exhilaration of the moment. As I lie here now I re-experience that feeling – the racing pulse, the desire to laugh and to shout for joy.

To fix that sensation in my subconscious mind, I take my right hand and place the tips of my thumb and first finger together. Now I do the same with my left hand. Gently but firmly I press and release these fingertips three times.

Now, still feeling very, very relaxed, I change the visualization to one where I am sitting at my own desk in a solicitor's office. On the desk are legal documents, some bound in red ribbon. On a shelf behind me are legal reference books. Sitting opposite me at the desk is a person whom I know to be a client I have been helping. I see that person smiling and leaning across the desk to shake my hand and thank me for all I have done.

I know I have used my skills to the best of my ability and that I have been successful. I know I am happy and fulfilled in the work I am doing. Still keeping that image in mind, I press together the tips of my thumbs and forefingers three times, thereby recalling immediately the 'wow' feeling of joy, excitement and exhilaration.

Helpful affirmations
- I can attain my goals.
- Positive success is mine.
- Wow!

11

Step By Step to Self-hypnosis

HOW TO USE THE SCRIPTS

It is possible to read and learn the scripts, or ask someone else to read to you. But the best way is to record on audio cassette.

(IMPORTANT: *Never practise self-hypnosis or listen to your script while driving or operating machinery.*)

Consider where you are now. List your likes and dislikes, then decide: what you need to change; and what you want to change. Think about what has made you the way you are now.

IMAGINATION AND VISUALIZATION

We are all born with the ability to visualize well, unless born blind. If you feel you have lost this ability, spend time relearning it by practising the exercises in chapter two. Ask yourself, 'What does "success" mean to me?' Learn to fool your subconscious mind, which cannot tell the difference between real and imagined experiences. Remember the importance of personalising your scripts.

YOUR STARTING POINT

Learn to relax:
• Choose a regular place and time.

- Go through the stages of physical relaxation concentrating on your breathing pattern, imagining yourself growing heavier.
- Avoid barriers to self-hypnosis such as being too analytical, too self-critical or becoming anxious about possible emergencies.
- Practise the deepening techniques until you find the best one for you.

AFFIRMATIONS

These only need to consist of a few words and need repetition, either vocally or by frequent reading.

GIVING UP SMOKING

The desire to quit must exist and the reasons must be yours. Perhaps:
- Health
- Money
- Smell
- Unsociable habit

Find your personal trigger and become aware of when it arises. Deal with the following aspects of smoking:
- Desire
- Habit
- Addiction

LOSING WEIGHT

Decide whether your weight problem arises through over-eating or whether it is really masking a deep emotional problem. Don't impose a 'diet' on yourself or you will give in the first day you feel negative. Remember the three rules:
- Only weigh yourself once a week.
- If you are hungry, you must eat.

- If you are not hungry, you must not eat anything.

If you reach a plateau in your weight loss, use the second script.

ONGOING PROBLEMS

There is a difference between a small amount of stress, which can be beneficial, and excess stress, which does great harm. Ongoing problems that can be alleviated by self-hypnosis include:

- Insomnia
- Asthma
- Migraine
- PMT/menopause
- Pain relief in certain circumstances – but only when the cause of the pain is known and your medical practitioner assures you that you can do yourself no harm by relieving that pain.

FEARS AND PHOBIAS

All fears and phobias will get worse unless dealt with – they never remain the same. Phobias can be:

- inherited;
- the result of an earlier event;
- have a basis in reality (fear of fire, flying, and so on).

There are three types of phobia sufferer and it is important to know which you are:

- Those who don't know and don't care how the phobia arose.
- Those who are aware of its cause.
- Those who don't know how the phobia arose but have a strong desire to find out (this requires the help of a professional and should not be tackled alone).

Always take things one stage at a time and refrain from trying to complete the change all at once.

EMOTIONAL PROBLEMS

Relationships
Your attitude towards others will have been formed in your early childhood and you will have a tendency to follow the pattern until you make a conscious decision to change. You need to:
• look back to discover how your attitude arose;
• forgive those who caused it;
• recognize the old pattern should it start to recur.

Bereavement
There are three stages that need to be recognized:
• Sadness – a natural reaction that is helped by time as you get used to the situation.
• Anger.
• Guilt – for things done or not done, said or not said.

Use self-hypnosis to complete 'unfinished business' and to help you understand and deal with other people's reactions to your bereavement. Feelings of guilt may be for past errors of omission or commission, and can be dealt with in three stages:
• make reparation where possible;
• learn from your mistake/s;
• forgive yourself.

PERFORMANCE UNDER PRESSURE

Sport
Using a hero/heroine as an imaginary mentor in your visualization enables you to give your very best performance.

Job interview
After doing your background research on the organization, visualizing yourself acting and speaking exactly as you would wish to during the interview (though it cannot guarantee you are offered the position) will ensure you acquit yourself well and have nothing to reproach yourself for.

Driving test

Visualize yourself taking the test and doing everything perfectly.

Examinations

When learning and revising:

- Select the relevant keywords.
- Imagine them being written slowly, letter by letter, so you can learn each set.
  Dealing with the exam itself:
- Visualize the place
- See yourself taking the exam, from the moment of turning over the paper to the moment of putting down your pen. Concentrate on relaxation before starting.
- Avoid post mortems.

MAKING YOUR FUTURE

Ensure you have dealt with outstanding problems first, then choose your direction by:

- making lists of hopes, fears, likes, interests and so on, then using self-hypnosis to allow your subconscious t show you the way;
- if there is a choice to be made, allow the imaginary video cassettes to play and show you the outcome.

Confidence and Self-esteem

Combine the image of your future goal with your experience of the 'wow' feeling from a past event.

Self-hypnosis cassettes are available from:

The Hypnothink Foundation
PO Box 66
Gloucester
GL2 9YG
UK
www.hypnothink.com/

Index

achievement 27–8, 41–2, 61, 133
addiction 51, 52, 136
adrenaline 81, 82
advertising 13, 42
affairs 100, 103
affirmations 13, 41–3, 136
  driving tests 120
  examinations 124
  fear of flying 99
  future goals 134
  giving up smoking 51
  guilt 112
  inherited phobias 93
  thunderstorms 93
  weight loss 66–7
agoraphobia 25–30
aids 97–8
airports 96–7
alcohol 64, 75, 97, 99
allergies 77, 79
altered states 32
anchoring 51, 97
anger 107, 138
anorexia 58
answer machines 34
apologies 110, 113
aptitudes 128
asthma 12, 71, 77–9, 137
aversion therapy 88
awareness 14, 103
babies 37
backache 83, 85
barriers 136
  giving up smoking 53–4
  relaxation 36–7
bereavement 12, 105–10, 138
blood pressure 39
booking tickets 96
boys 89–90, 93
brain capacity 121
brain waves 32
breathing 35, 40, 50, 77–9
bulimia 58
calories 60–1, 64, 69
carbohydrates 61, 69
cards 42
case studies 7
  affirmations 42–3
  bereavement 107–8
  driving tests 119–20
  examinations 125–6

fear of flying 95, 97–8
future plans 129–30
giving up smoking 57
guilt 112–14
insomnia 76
pain-relief 85
parent-child relationships 100–2
success 25–8
targets 30
weight loss 59–60
cassettes 12, 14, 36–7
  fear of flying 98
  giving up smoking 51–2, 54
  insomnia 76
  recording 14
  relaxation 39–41
  safety 7–8, 38–9
  slowing down 36
  suppliers 140
  using 7, 12, 135
categories 18–19, 91
chairs 34
change 15–19, 135
chewing gum 53
childbirth 12
childhood experiences 9–10, 138
  emotional difficulties 100–5
  future goals 131–2
  imagination 12
  phobias 89–90
choices 130–1
Christie, Linford 22–3, 116
claustrophobia 25, 95
clothing 34
coffee 75, 79
cold turkey 45
comfort 34
commitment 15, 48, 128
concentration 12, 15–16, 35, 39–41
confidence 7, 12, 17, 25, 27
  dating 30
  future plans 131–4, 139
  performance 118
conscious 9–11, 14, 18
  affirmations 43
  future plans 127–8
  relaxation 33, 36
constipation 83
counting breaths 35
cowardice 87, 90
cravings 60

creativity 22
dating 30
daydreams 31
death 105–10, 138
deepening techniques 37–8, 41, 136
dehydration 97
deprivation 62–3, 68–70
desensitization 96
design 31
desire 51, 52, 136
diarrhoea 83
diets 60–1, 69, 125
dislikes 83, 128, 135
doctors 8, 58, 64
    emotional difficulties 101
    ongoing problems 81–3, 85
doubt 131–3
drama 115
drinking 64, 68, 75, 97
driving 7, 14, 38–9
driving tests 28, 115, 119–20, 139
eating
    disorders 58
    habits 60–4
    plans 62–4, 69–70
eczema 73
Edison, Thomas 128
education 20–1
Einstein, Albert 128
emergencies 37
emotional difficulties 58, 138
    ongoing problems 77
    self-help 100–14
    weight 59–60
emphysema 46–7
epilepsy 8, 12
examinations 12, 42–3, 139
    performance 115, 120–6
    phobias 90
exercises 21–2, 78–9
experiments 10–11, 15
failure 23, 69–70
fears 12, 25, 87–99, 128
    flying 42, 88, 90, 95–9, 137
    future goals 137, 139
    subconscious 28–9
feathers 87, 88
fire 95
fixing technique 50–2, 78, 97–9
fizzy drinks 64
fluids 64
flying 25, 42, 88, 90, 95–9
food 60–1
forbidden foods 61
forgiveness 103–5, 110–14, 138

frequently-asked questions 11–12
friends 48–9, 54
future plans 127–34, 139
garments 34
genetics 18
girls 89–90, 93
giving up smoking 9, 12, 42, 44–57, 136
goals 131–3
grief 105–10, 138
guilt 59–60, 107–14, 138
habits 14–15, 19, 21
    eating 60–4
    sleeping 74–5
    smoking 44, 50–4, 136
headaches 42, 79–81, 82, 83
health 46, 53–4, 74
hearing 13–14
heart attacks 46
heart rate 39
heaviness 35–6, 38, 40–1
hopes 128, 139
hormone replacement therapy (HRT) 82
hormones 81–2
hospitalization 77, 85
hot flushes 82
HRT *see* hormone replacement therapy
hunger 62–4, 66, 68, 136
hyperventilation 77–8
hypnotherapy 9, 11, 18, 77
    emotional difficulties 101
    performance 116
    phobias 91, 94
    starting 32, 34
Hypnothink Foundation 140
hysterectomy 85
hysteria 90
imagination 13, 20–31, 135
improving imagination 21–2
induction technique 12, 37
    deepening 37–8
    driving tests 120
    emotional difficulties 104
    examinations 121
    future plans 130–1
    heaviness 36
    ongoing problems 72, 80
    script 39–41
    smoking 55
    weight loss 67
inhalers 77
inherited phobias 89, 91–3
insomnia 7, 74–6, 137

interviews 12, 115, 118, 138
intuition 127
Jacobs, David 106
job interviews 12, 115, 118, 138
keywords 120–2, 139
ladders 95
life-threatening conditions 58
likes 128, 135, 139
lists 16–17, 128–9, 135, 139
location 34, 123
lung cancer 46
machine use 8, 38
marketing 13
materialism 24, 25
medication 76, 77, 99
memory 12, 20
menopause 12, 81–2, 137
menstruation 81–2
mental rehearsal 24, 26–7
mentors 117–18, 138
metabolism 64
migraine 12, 71, 79–81
mirrors 66, 68
money 24, 25, 47
moving 36–7
nail-biting 7
negativity 13, 15, 17, 19
    emotional difficulties 105, 112
    imagination 23, 31
nervousness 12, 24–5, 115
    performance 119–20, 123
    smoking 49
nicotine 45–6, 52, 54
noise 34
note-taking 120–1
ongoing problems 71–86
operations 85
other people 34, 48–9, 54, 109–10, 125
pain 35, 39, 81–5
panic attacks 12, 77–8
paraphernalia 54
parent-child relationships 9–10,
    89–90, 100–5, 131–2, 138
past experiences 9–10, 89–90, 100–5,
    131–2, 138
people categories 18–19, 91
performance pressures 115–26, 138–9
personality 16–19
phobias 7, 12, 87–99, 137
    case study 25–7
    subconscious 28–9
physical relaxation 35–9
place 34, 123
plane tickets 96
planning 14

plateau weight 67–8, 137
PMT *see* premenstrual tension
positivity 13, 15, 17–18
    affirmations 42–3
    guilt 114
    sport 116–17
    visualization 23
post mortems 125, 126, 139
post-it notes 42, 43
practising 41
pregnancy 12
premenstrual tension (PMT) 12, 71,
    81–2, 137
preparation 34, 135–6
pressure cookers 72
pressure of performance 115–26,
    138–9
programming 9–10, 14
psoriasis 73
psychological coaches 116
public transport 47
pulse rate 39
questions 11–12
reading 13–14
regular practice 33–4
rehearsal 24, 26–7
reinforcement 9–10, 23, 26
    fears 87
    phobias 90
    smoking 48, 54
    sport 117
relationships 17, 100–5, 138
relaxation 8–9, 12, 32–4, 50–1
    asthma 78
    deepening 37–8, 41, 136
    examinations 121
    exercise 55
    fear of flying 96–9
    future plans 130–1
    migraine 80
    physical 35–9
    safety 38–9
    scripts 39–41, 67, 128
    stages 135–6
    stress 71
repetition 13, 16, 42, 88
resistance 15
retirement 129
revision 42–3, 120–1
role models 117
routines 74–5
rules 61–7, 68, 136
sadness 106, 138
safety 7–8, 38–9
scales 62, 64, 67

scripts 7
  bereavement 108
  cassettes 37
  design 31
  emotional difficulties 60
  examinations 121–2, 123–4
  fear of flying 96–9
  forgiveness 104–5, 110
  future goals 133–4
  giving up smoking 49–50, 52, 54–7
  guilt 111–12
  in-flight 98–9
  inherited phobias 91–3
  insomnia 75, 125
  job interviews 118
  known cause 93–4
  migraine 80, 81
  pain relief 81–4
  phobias 91
  reading 34, 37
  relaxation 33, 39–41, 67, 128
  sport 117, 118
  stress 72–3, 77, 79, 81–2
  using 7, 135
  weight loss 65–9
seeing 13–14, 21–2
self-esteem 131–4, 139
self-talk 12–14
setting dates 96–7
Shakespeare, William 128
shyness 17, 30
sins of omission/commission 110, 138
skills 128
sleep 10, 11, 33, 74–6, 125, 128
slip-ups 69–70
slowing down 36
smell 47–8
smoking 9, 12, 42, 44–57, 136
snakes 83
social acceptance 47
soul 106
spiders 19, 28–9, 83
spiritualism 106
sport 22–4, 29, 115, 116–18, 138
stage hypnotists 8
stress 12, 76–7
  excess 71–4, 79, 82–3
  future goals 137
  ongoing problems 79, 81–2
  relaxation 39–41
  smoking 45
strokes 46
studying 42–3, 120–1
subconscious 9–11, 14, 18–19

affirmations 43
examinations 123
fear of flying 96–7
fooling 28–9
future goals 127–9, 131, 134, 139
giving up smoking 52
imagination 23, 26, 135
insomnia 75
phobias 87–8
relaxation 32–3, 36, 50
weight loss 59, 65–6
success 24–30, 61
suppliers 140
talking 12–14, 36
tar 56
target-setting 29–30, 96–7
team sport 116, 118
teeth-grinding 83
telephones 34
television 33, 34, 75
temperature 34
tests 115
theatres 47
therapy 8–9
thunderstorms 89, 92–3
timing 33–4
tinnitus 71, 73
training 36
trance 32, 38
trauma 77, 87–99
triggers 49, 50–1, 136
ulcers 83
unfinished business 108–9, 138
visualizations 13, 20–31
  driving tests 120
  examinations 121–4
  fear of flying 96–7
  future goals 132–4
  future plans 135
  inherited phobias 92–3
  pain relief 83–4
  weight loss 64–5, 66
vitamins 125
water 64
web site 140
weighing 62, 64–6, 68, 136
weight 9, 12, 29
  gain 53, 59, 61
  loss 58–70, 136–7
willpower 9, 11–12
withdrawal symptoms 45
worms 89, 93–4
"wow" moments 132–3, 139
yoga 12, 35, 38